# PERT:

# A NEW MANAGEMENT
# PLANNING AND
# CONTROL TECHNIQUE

# CONTRIBUTORS

*E. T. Alsaker*

*William Bloom*

*Ernest O. Codier*

*Walter Cosinuke*

*Harold G. Francis*

*Charles W. Getz*

*Leonard P. Hartung*

*G. Truman Hunter*

*Donald G. Malcolm*

*Austin McHugh*

*George T. Mundorff*

*Kenneth M. Tebo*

# EDITOR

*Jerome W. Blood*

# PERT

## A NEW MANAGEMENT PLANNING AND CONTROL TECHNIQUE

*By Gabriel N. Stilian and Others*

AMERICAN MANAGEMENT ASSOCIATION
NEW YORK

Third Printing

This is No. 74 in the series of AMA Management Reports.

# FOREWORD

**W**E HAVE SEEN tremendous strides made in the development of the profession of scientific management and of management skills. Each of us, as an individual manager, has been able to make some—and perhaps frequent—contributions to the present and future well-being of his particular company. Not so frequently, however, have we had the opportunity to develop a management technique of such wide scope that it is potentially valuable to companies of all sizes and in all kinds of industries.

In the case of PERT we do have such a technique, and it has been satisfying to me personally for AMA to have had the opportunity to take a major role in introducing and developing PERT as a general management tool. Having realized the great management value of the original work done by Admiral William F. Raborn in using PERT for the Polaris program, the Administrative Services Division of AMA designed a series of programs to apply PERT management systems to the needs of business for all types of management functions and programs for which PERT concepts were applicable.

When PERT is used properly, the results can be truly significant. This is so because for the first time we have a means of achieving accuracy in the planning and control of activities which were heretofore not amenable to such precision. We now have in PERT—as, earlier, in the Gantt chart—the basis for a valuable management tool with possibilities for wide-scale application.

However, this tool is only in the incubation stage. It will take much creative thinking, much development, and much company experience to invest it with the full usefulness of which it appears to be capable. It therefore behooves every professional manager to participate in the development of this technique wherever he may be using it. It is for this reason that this AMA book has been written, and I hope that it will help introduce PERT to many thousands of executives for their serious consideration.

> LAWRENCE A. APPLEY
> *President*
> *American Management Association*

# CONTENTS

# AUTHOR'S NOTE

One of the important concepts that has been developed by AMA in recent years has been the management-information-systems approach to executive decision making. The initial work included the well-known AMA business simulation game. With this and other experiences as background, AMA was able to collaborate with leaders in the field in developing the computer as a management tool. PERT is one of many management information and control systems which follow this approach—and one of the most valuable.

In its work on PERT, AMA found that some of the concepts that are the elements of PERT—such as network analysis—apply to simple, short-range problems as well as to the more complicated problems which PERT has usually been associated with. Hence this book, along with the many programs on PERT offered by AMA, emphasizes the methodology and concepts of systems which may not be considered by technicians to be "pure" PERT technique. The important thing is that the executive in business have available an effective method of making a profit for his company by doing a better management job. We hope that this book will start the reader in this direction; if it does so, it will have accomplished its purpose.

I wish to thank the other authors for the important role they played in helping AMA to achieve the objectives of this book as well as for their extensive work in the preparation of their chapters.

G.N.S.

# AN OVER-ALL VIEW OF PERT •

CHARLES W. GETZ

N O OTHER MANAGEMENT TOOL in recent years has had so much written about it, been the subject of so many speeches, or had such publicity as PERT (Program Evaluation and Review Technique). At last count there were over 400 manuals, magazine articles, papers, and dissertations published on this method with the catchy name. Yet, despite this widespread publicity, PERT is still very poorly understood. Its notoriety has led managers to expect miracles, to think of PERT as a panacea, and to assume that if a man is not PERTing, he is not managing.

Simply put, PERT is a planning technique and tool of management control which uses network theory. A plan is a map of the future. As a planning technique, PERT is a most valuable service. It is a method for drawing this map. If management used nothing of the technique except network preparation—even without time estimates—then it would gain significant benefit from its use. Some industry representatives estimate this to be 70 to 90 per cent of the value of the technique. But management does not have to stop there: PERT is a fine tool of management control, and it is also a good prognostic medium.

THE ORIGINS OF PERT

We must first of all understand that network theory is not a new concept. Scientists and engineers have been using it for centuries, but it is customary today when tracing the history of network theory, particularly PERT, to start with Henry Laurence Gantt. This doesn't mean that there is nothing new in what was originally called PERT. On the contrary, the original PERT technique did make novel contributions.

PERT is a mixture of new ideas and proven experience. For example, the three time estimates of PERT are a new concept. Their use in

CHARLES W. GETZ is Assistant to the Director of Management Controls, Lockheed Missiles & Space Company, Sunnyvale, California.

probability computation is of comparatively lesser significance (and a subject of intense controversy). This is also new. The three time estimates put realism into R&D schedules. This is perhaps PERT's major contribution to management planning. A major advance was made when a method to show the uncertainty of future R&D schedules was developed. Before PERT, R&D people were requested to pick a specific *point in time,* several years ahead, when they were going to invent something. Now, they are asked to estimate a *period of time.*

One of the major reasons network theory has become so popular is the fact that so many people recognize the technique. The project engineer does not see anything revolutionary in networking because he has always thought in those same well-ordered, interdependent terms while planning his programs. He has been trained to orderly thinking. For this reason, many experienced project engineers do not understand all the fuss being made about PERT.

On the other hand, the industrial engineers believe they invented network theory, and to some degree this is correct. PERT is related in many ways to the industrial engineer's process flow chart. Industrial engineers point out the fact that part of the line of balance chart uses networking theory and that it was in use by the Goodyear Company before World War II.

The mathematician instantly recognizes the topological approach in the PERT network. The mathematics of PERT alone have been the subject of many papers and debates. PERT may not be good mathematics, but it is good management.

Talk to the production scheduler, and he will claim that networking is merely an offshoot of production scheduling sheets and production control charts. He acknowledges Gantt as his "founding father"— together with Frederick W. Taylor. Some of the earliest work in network theory began as papers on production scheduling.

The Air Force weapon-system director will tell you that weapon-systems management as practiced in the Air Force for the past 15 years has concentrated on the many parts, the composite of which forms a total weapon system. Networks merely graph this relationship.

All of these people are right, to a degree, which is one of the advantages of the technique; it is not overly difficult to explain or sell it to engineers, schedulers, and other people whose jobs require the logical planning of interrelated parts.

As a matter of historical record, the Navy began to use PERT in the management of the Polaris program early in 1959. The Air Force interest in the technique also dates from this period, although Air Force use of PERT did not start until late 1959. In 1956 the Navy Special Project Office began to look around for ideas on management control: within the Navy, in private industry, and in the Air Force ballistic missile program. Because of the similarities in problems, the Navy adopted many of the techniques of control then being used in the ballistic missile program, such as the control room, milestone charts, and the Commander's Conference (the well-known "Black Saturday" meetings).

PERT SYNONYMOUS WITH PLANNING

The prime, most basic, and singularly important record in a weapon system development program is undoubtedly the schedule record. All other records stem from this one. Schedule records are of value in the two areas of planning and control; and of these two, the planning function is the more important. Slippages, overruns, and overcomplication are just a few of the myriad of program problems that have their beginning in the planning stage. PERT is primarily a tool of planning and, as such, makes its greatest contribution at that stage.

PERT forces logical thought. It compels program planners to recognize the relationship of the parts to the whole; because of this, PERT is a natural as a weapon-system planning tool. However, it is certainly not limited to this use. In fact, whenever anything must be planned and is of sufficient complexity to warrant being put on a piece of paper, PERT provides a better way to do it.

The use of the network is a somewhat controversial subject that needs some clarification. In a large project which requires computerization of the PERT data (and under most conditions), the project manager—after a network has been satisfactorily drawn, reworked, and received his approval—will be better off if he does not use it again until he must replan in whole or in part. He should let PERT reports or PERT-derived reports do the control job. A PERT network is like a map; once the route is drawn, we can more easily follow progress against a checklist of keypoints or milestones (PERT management reports). Many operating managers become frustrated and disillusioned with PERT because staff people try to force them to use the network as a series of progress reports. It is true that in some instances project engineers do like to use the network as a progress-reporting or recording tool since it is more akin to blueprints than machine-prepared reports, but this is a matter of preference and certainly should not be rigidly determined. However, using the network to follow the progress of a large program is the exception and not the rule.

VALUE TO LINE MANAGEMENT

Despite the widespread use of PERT and the aggressive pursuit of newer and better methods of application, PERT has been received by line management with mixed emotions and varying success.

If line management has sometimes been less than enthusiastic about PERT, it may be because PERT has a tendency to gravitate away from line management into the hands of support management. There are plenty of reasons for this situation:

1. Data-systems designers and operators are overcomplicating and oversophisticating the PERT system.
2. Network preparation is delegated to people who are not project-oriented.
3. The mechanics of the system are dominating the most important aspect of PERT, which is the project-level planning (networking) by personnel who will carry out the plan.
4. Project management does not exert its leadership responsibilities over support functions.
5. So many other complexities, both real and imagined, frustrate today's line managers that they are more than willing to rid themselves of detailed tasks.
6. Some line managers fear that PERT will be used as a whip and not as an aid. There is already evidence to substantiate this fear.
7. Analysis is most generally handled by the PERT staff instead of by the line management responsible for the job. It is only when reports are in the hands of management that real results and discipline are achieved.
8. Finally, PERT is sometimes forced upon project management. Although some reasonable and general compulsion may be justifiable, direct ultimatums seldom succeed.

If we must admit—after discounting the exuberance of many users—

that in some cases no spectacular results have been observed and that programs still have slippages and overruns, it may be because we have forgotten that management success is primarily the result of managerial competence rather than of any particular management tool—including PERT—that is employed.

The implications for top management would seem obvious. PERT has proved itself in specific instances to be too valuable a management tool to be denied to line management, and those conditions which inhibit its use by line managers must be removed. Further, top management must be convinced that PERT, like any management tool, is only as effective as the man who uses it.

PROMISE FOR THE FUTURE

Certain it is that PERT or, more correctly, the network analysis technique has opened the door to a better understanding of management systems. The networking theory is awakening managers to the many interrelated complexities of business operations. A management system is composed of equipment, skills, procedures, and techniques—the composite of which forms an instrument of administration or control. Just as equipment, training manuals, skilled personnel, facilities, and so forth are essential parts of a missile system, so too are these things a part of a management system. Networks developed today for programs are now beginning to include a greater number of administrative actions, paperwork, and decision points. Eventually, managers will be able to plot on networks most organizational functions that may be planned in the future, including such routine matters as the setting up of financial targets, the scheduling of recurring reports and meetings, and labor-contract negotiations.

By using automated control information, management will be alerted when even these routine functions are not being carried out according to plan. In other words, network techniques will provide a true means for identifying exceptions so that we can manage by exception. Many supervisors *claim* they manage by exception, but they have no way of identifying the exceptions. Undoubtedly, the increased awareness of management systems and the increased use of network theory in general administration will be one of the most significant outgrowths of present PERT applications.

# SECTION I: PERT AND THE MANAGER

*In today's competitive business environment the demands made on the manager's time and skill are increasing. At a time when business operations have reached an unparalleled degree of complexity and the maintenance of profit margins has become a major problem, he is being asked to perform his job with even greater precision and effectiveness. New management methods and tools have been developed to aid him in the everyday task of planning and controlling his work. Among these tools, the PERT technique is beginning to stand out as one of the most valuable and promising.*

# NEW TOOLS IN THE GROWING
# MANAGEMENT TECHNOLOGY •

DONALD G. MALCOLM

---

DURING THE PAST dozen years, a number of significant developments in management methods have occurred. Progressive, competitive managements have been quick to realize and utilize the better decision making and managerial control made possible by the electronic computer, programed with advanced management systems and used in conjunction with mathematical modeling.

These new management methods show promise of becoming an important competitive element in industry as well as valuable contributors to defense programs. A company's success or failure may stem directly from its ability to understand quickly and utilize effectively these new concepts in daily operations and planning. Techniques such as PERT/Time, PERT/Cost, PERT/Reliability, the critical path method, and line of balance are examples of these new tools.

There are three main reasons why these new methods are desirable and useful to management. First, there is a continuing need to improve the efficiency of operations through quicker, more responsive, and more integrated controls and, especially, to see tangible results from the investment in data processing. Second, management wishes to improve its ability to identify problems in advance by looking ahead rather than relying in the main on approaches that discover deviations from plan after the fact and then attempt to prevent recurrences in the future. Third, in coping with the R&D process, management in both the military and industry are faced with the necessity of reducing the time and cost of development programs. The company that can more quickly turn the

---

DONALD G. MALCOLM is President, Management Technology Inc., Los Angeles, California.

fruits of R&D efforts into useful and desired products can gain market initiative.

Dramatic new tools for management are emerging. As we learn to use them, we will improve communications, streamline our organizations, acquire the capability to link our planning and operations functions more effectively, and be able to simulate the effect of proposed plans or changes in plans on our cost, time, and product-performance objectives *before* taking action or enunciating policy. The total management problem will become visible. Although the road ahead is beset with many pitfalls, a few guiding principles have emerged:

1. Management systems must be designed and implemented in the same careful, systematic manner that has gradually become standard practice in the design and development of hardware items.

2. A program for management-system development—involving indoctrination and training, system descriptions, and training manuals—is essential.

3. Top management support, organizational status for the systems-design function, and competent engineers must be provided to insure the success of management-system programs.

Developments in science and technology have resulted in projects of unprecedented size and complexity. We have attempted to reduce or compress the time required to complete these programs by adopting the principle of concurrency—that is, the simultaneous design and development of major weapon systems—and by broad innovations in our organizational approach to the problem. Improvements in the day-to-day management of these projects—many of which involve systems engineering—have not kept pace with scientific growth. Systems engineering techniques have not been widely used in the management of our projects. PERT and its extensions have been conceived in part as tools which will help control and reduce the costs of such concurrency programs.

Moreover, there are two major problems inherent in the information flow of many large projects:

1. The flow often takes too long to pass through the various levels of the organization. Each level interprets and analyzes the information before passing it along, which results in defensive interpretations and a lack of integrity in the data that reach the higher levels.

2. Information is summarized in functional form—that is, it is

collected by each organizational function. Quite often the information is adjusted to agree with the budgets of these functions and is not in accord with the project character of the work.

Methods of information flow that cut across the functional lines of activities and focus upon program objectives and provide a speedy flow of information in a channel outside the normal organizational pattern have become necessary. The Polaris program of the Navy, for example, demonstrated that it was possible to design a system of information which had its roots in subprojects and could be drawn off at the various levels of the organization without destroying the command structure necessary to effective management.

In the activities for which management is responsible, three factors are paramount: *time, resources,* and *performance.* Management uses information in planning, executing, and controlling these activities. Management systems help establish plans leading to goals, measure progress toward the goals, and indicate problems involved in achieving the goals. PERT and its extensions are tools designed to assist management in this job.

Experts in the field often speak of "generations" of missiles, each generation having a greater range or other operational capability than the preceding ones. The same concept of going at it in a series of generations has been applied to management systems. The first generation of PERT tackled the problem of *time* in development programs. Second and third generations of PERT are concerned with *costs* and *reliability.*

PERT/TIME

In the PERT/Time approach, a development program is first portrayed graphically as a network of interrelated activities necessary to achieve prescribed events. Events are shown as squares or rectangles in the diagram and activities as the connecting arrows. The critical path is the longest path through a particular program. It is this part of the program that management is most anxious to determine, shorten, and monitor.

The relationship of the network approach of PERT and traditional Gantt charting is worth commenting on. In Gantt charting, no dependency or interconnection between activities is shown, and coordinate functions and precedent relationships are not shown. These are of major significance in large R&D programs where many activities must be performed concurrently and coordinated properly. Planning for these points and utilizing the resulting plan in monitoring make it more nearly possible to "create on schedule." The use of the network is thus a significant innovation in the body of industrial engineering techniques.

The next step in the PERT process is to obtain elapsed-time estimates for each activity in the network from engineers responsible for their completion. The three estimates—optimistic, most likely, and pessimistic—obtained for each activity represent the range of time which can be expected. They are, in turn, transformed into a probability statement indicating the chances of the activity taking different lengths of time to be achieved.

The flow plan and time estimates are then fed into a computer which sorts out the longest path from all the possible paths. All other paths to an event are said to have slack in them, and they represent areas where resources may possibly be reallocated. The path having zero slack is, therefore, the critical path. Thus PERT aids management by exception because it tells the manager where slips are likely to occur and what their magnitude may be. It also indicates where slack exists in the program and is a guide for reallocating some of the resources to reduce total program time. This identification of slack areas also tells the manager where *not* to buy attractive time reduction opportunities.

PERT is maintained and updated according to a regular plan (see Exhibit 1). Another feature of PERT is the possibility of simulating a change. The manager can introduce a synthetic time reduction and find out what would happen to the total program as a result. Changes often do not bring about a time reduction in the program and have to be rejected. In addition, many displays are possible from the data available in the PERT computer files. A variety of reports can be adapted to individual management needs and preferences. It is highly important for management to specify what it wants out of the computer and not vice versa. It frequently happens that the computer facility can see many possibilities of analyses and outputs of interest to it, which merely complicate the situation and make it difficult for management to see the real simplicity of the PERT technique.

A management systems-design function is being established in many companies to serve as a sort of buffer between management and the computer facility. The specialists in this function know the needs of

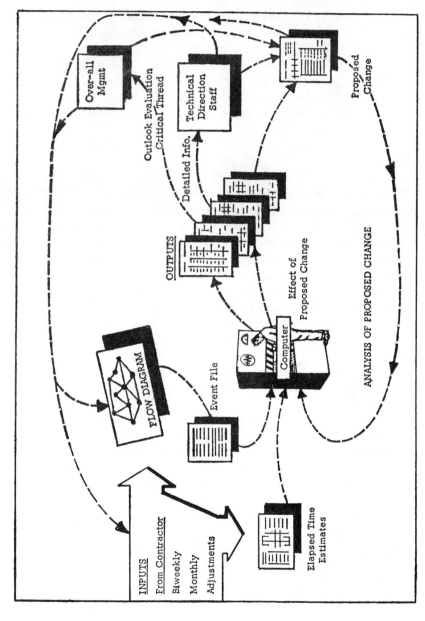

PERT SYSTEM IN OPERATION

EXHIBIT 1

management and are also able to communicate effectively with the computer experts. The role of the systems designer is becoming better recognized as the need for improved management controls is realized in companies. Many requests for proposals which are issued by military organizations require that the management controls which are to be employed be set forth in the proposal. As a result, systems designers are now free to choose appropriate types of organization, reporting channels, information-gathering techniques, and computer programs for evaluating alternatives at decision points.

PERT/COST

Early in the original PERT research, it was deemed impractical on two counts to cope simultaneously with all three variables (time, cost, and performance) in a computer model. First, related cost and time data on activities not experienced before are almost impossible to obtain with any degree of accuracy. Further data on costs and time for different degrees of the item's performance are even more difficult to obtain. Second, even if the data were obtainable, roughly 20 times the amount required by the basic PERT system would be necessary. Therefore, it was reasoned that if an integrated time-cost-performance approach were taken at the outset, the cost and data problem would hinder acceptance by the potential user of the system. Because time was of the essence in the Polaris project, the Navy decided to tackle the time variable first and go on to costs after the information channels had been established.

There are a number of ways costs can be assigned to activities. A range of possible costs can be applied to each activity, or a single cost for each one of the time estimates in PERT can be made. Moreover, we must decide whether to use a single cost, direct costs, or total costs. PERT applications have generally applied direct man-hour costs, either in man-hours or dollars, to the activity showing the department code for the man. In many cases, the individual man is identified, especially where highly skilled personnel are a scarce commodity in great demand.

We have a problem in making PERT cost data compatible with fiscal practices already in effect. Planned activities often cut across the orderly monthly accounting periods. It is possible to convert from PERT activities to financial planning and accounting by knowing the rate of expenditure, but it is not possible to work in the other direction in the absence of a PERT diagram. In short, PERT costs should be considered an input to current accounting systems. The following output reports can then be made available by a PERT/Cost system:

1. Expected manpower needs by skill, month, and department.
2. Individual man loading by month.
3. Expected project direct costs by skill, month, and department.
4. Regular PERT/Time outputs: slack areas, critical paths, expected calendar time, and impact prediction.

PERT costs and budgeted costs may not always agree. PERT costs will usually be lower and displaced in time because of the fact that all direct work may not be easily identified with networked activities.

After the first PERT cost outputs are available and management has used them in improving utilization and balancing the workload, other opportunities to reallocate resources to activities or to apply new resources will appear. The effect of these in regard to the over-all schedule, or time objective, may be easily evaluated by a simulated change, with the increment costs known. The effectiveness can be measured in terms of the time reduction to be achieved. In the course of planning any project, there will be peaks and valleys in the requirements for the services of individual skills and individuals in particular. Where knowledge of this can be ascertained in advance, the time may be scheduled for other productive work that the company has available or desires to do—such as a directed research effort. In addition, this is a good project-control device for management.

In summary, cost outputs are being used in company planning for the following purposes:

1. Determining and improving utilization.
2. Balancing the workload.
3. Evaluating cost-time trade-offs.
4. Determining the percentage of directed work.
5. Scheduling of the manpower build-up.
6. Identifying and assigning technical work.

PERT/RELIABILITY

Two general approaches toward greater reliability have been adopted. The first approach attempts to put a numerical value on the expected operational reliability of the end item: by measurement or test, a number indicates how many times out of how many trials an item will perform as specified. This simple ratio is a measure of the reliability. The second approach tries to increase reliability by monitoring the documentation required as a part of good engineering practice. Under this method, the development plan is monitored to see that there is compliance with the basic design, the specifications, reliability-test procedures, acceptance-test procedures, and so forth. The theory is that proper compliance with these reliability-event documents will result in a more reliable product. The ratio of compliance is known as the reliability maturity index (RMI). In the RMI extension to PERT, two ratings for each reliability event are made: the technical quality evaluation (TQE) and schedule compliance evaluation (SCE). The average of these two ratings provides RMI.

TQE is an independent audit of the reliability-event documents to determine whether the required information has been adequately supplied. The TQE report is prepared by an engineer as he evaluates an activity that has culminated in a reliability event. An arithmetical process yields a number, between 0 and 100, which is TQE of the activity. The TQE report consists of two parts: a summary of weighted scoring and a discussion of weighting and scoring. Each item of an assembly is rated in accordance with the factors shown in Exhibit 2.

SCE provides the planning, scheduling, reporting, and monitoring functions of RMI. Two different SCE rating values are calculated for each assembly and its lower-level items: a relative composite rating and a cumulative composite rating. For each assembly an additional weighted rating calculation is made. The relative composite rating is derived by totaling the actual number of reliability-event documents completed as of the report's date and dividing by the number of reliability-event documents scheduled to have been completed *by that date*. The cumulative composite rating is derived by totaling the actual number of reliability-event documents completed as of the report's date and then dividing by the number of reliability events documents scheduled *for the total program*. The individual TQE ratings for each completed reliability-event document evaluated are transmitted by the evaluating personnel to those persons responsible for the SCE reporting function of RMI. In this funneling manner, a composite TQE rating is calculated for all TQE ratings derived up to a specified date.

RELIABILITY MATURITY INDEX

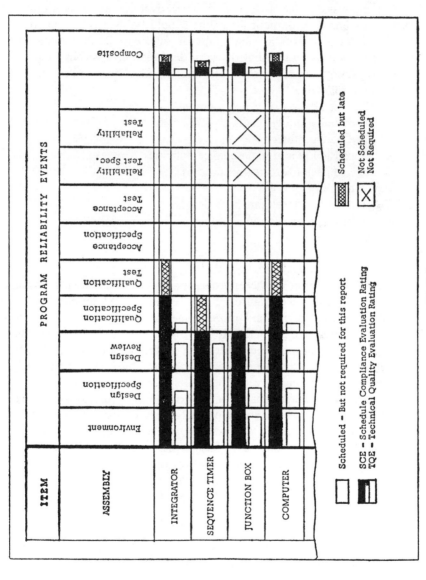

EXHIBIT 2

INDUSTRIAL APPLICATIONS OF PERT

The impression that PERT and its derivatives are useful only in large, one-time development programs should be dispelled. Networking has been found useful in small jobs of 5,000 to 20,000 man-hours. Several users have stated that the very discipline involved in such planning has prevented many errors. The approach has been utilized in areas such as the following:

1. The installation of a new computer.
2. The shelter program in civil defense.
3. The new-product process.
4. Construction and maintenance activities.
5. The financial forecasting process.
6. Mining operations.
7. Real estate development programs.
8. Highway construction.
9. Cost control.
10. Documentation control.
11. Value engineering.

A brief description of the approach being taken in the new products area will illustrate the nature of the approach. Although American industry is putting more and more money in research, it has a major problem in determining whether it is getting a payoff on this investment. Techniques for planning and controlling R&D functions are still embryonic in nature. A way to predict and plan for the timely and efficient exploitation of company research results is most needed.

There are three major phases in developing a new product—a process that takes an average of about 6 to 7 years in some industries (see Exhibit 3). First, there is the task of searching out ideas and doing fundamental research. The next phase is the broad area of development and test, where selected ideas are brought up to reality by means of a pilot product. Coordination with the other functional areas in the company is most important at this stage. Marketing, engineering, and manufacturing all become involved because each has an eventual responsibility. Finally, if the test product is deemed feasible, it is moved into the commercial phase, where it becomes a part of the product line. It is estimated that out of 400 or 500 ideas, only one or two ever reach this final phase.

THE NEW PRODUCT PROCESS

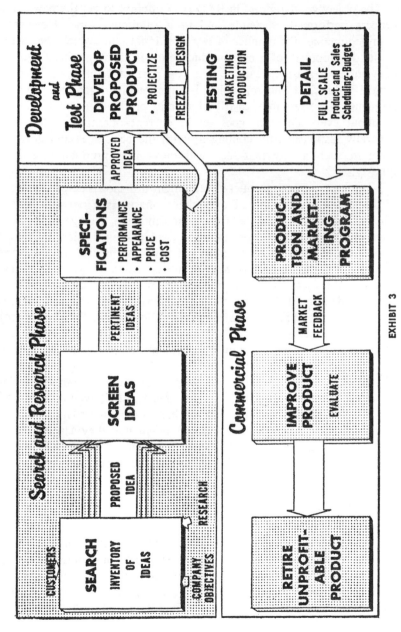

EXHIBIT 3

The objective, therefore, in R&D is to attempt to get the new product process performed efficiently and in a minimum time. However, in many companies the number of organizational units which are involved in the development of a new product tends to delay getting these products out in a reasonable time. The top part of Exhibit 4 illustrates a typical industrial concern, which is functionally organized. Top management, sales, research, distribution, and production—each has a say in about everything that goes on in current operations. Research is generally responsible for coming up with the new ideas and developing them in such a way that they will move into production and sales quickly.

The phases of new product development are shown across the bottom of Exhibit 4. Superimposed over these phases is a network diagram. The movement from left to right represents the passage of time. The lines which come down from the top in spider-web fashion indicate that almost all of the functional areas get involved in each of the various phases—and this is usually not in any coordinated way. The idea of creating a project management concept for the product early in the game and using PERT as the management tool to cut across the functional lines appears promising and follows logically after a project network is established. Thus, the use of the networking concept will have an effect on the traditional functional organization. Some refer to this as turning the organization 90 degrees and focusing on the project objectives. We need project managers who can reach out for the necessary staff and systems analysis. In this way the whole organization can be coordinated and brought to bear on new product objectives. Companies using this approach are confident that they can cut the time and cost of the development of new products by at least 20 per cent because of better coordination between the functional areas of the company at an earlier point in time.

THE TASK AHEAD

There is great opportunity to reduce data requirements for management through properly designed systems and to automate, to a degree, many of the routine analyses made by clerical personnel. Cost reduction opportunities are significant. The development of new display devices and management centers offers potential reductions in hard

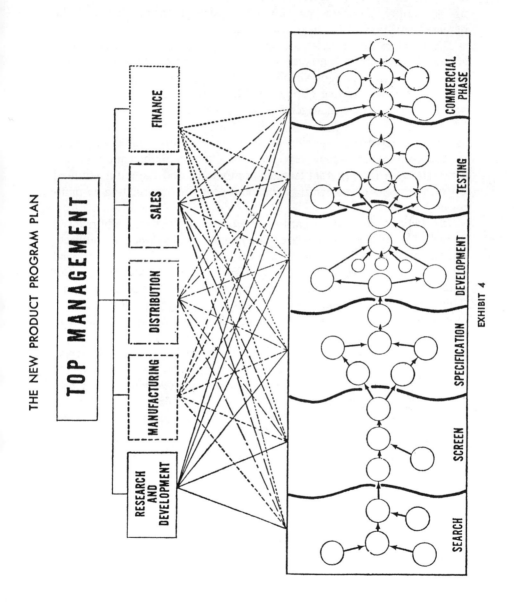

THE NEW PRODUCT PROGRAM PLAN

TOP MANAGEMENT

RESEARCH AND DEVELOPMENT · MANUFACTURING · DISTRIBUTION · SALES · FINANCE

SEARCH · SCREEN · SPECIFICATION · DEVELOPMENT · TESTING · COMMERCIAL PHASE

EXHIBIT 4

copy as well as easier access to the data bank. This will enhance the use and utility of systems and promises a very important change in the management tools in the next few years.

Displays are not a self-contained activity but a vital component of an over-all system, which consists of not only the PERT cycle but the total real-life program of which the PERT cycle is in itself a part. Hence, the most effective displays will be those that utilize the formats and terminology that management personnel are working with in real life and that are integrated with the PERT output displays. Displays should also have the capability of being used with equal effectiveness as the core of hard-copy reports. Thus, the communication format established for the program is made continuous, and the effort required by management to recognize significant program information is minimized.

In addition, the need for hard-copy reports will be drastically reduced as real-time management information systems are developed and utilized. Automated management control centers, such as those being developed or under way in the military, will permit managers from the various company functions to review program status and plans as a group. Thus, the seemingly endless coordination of staff reports will be avoided. When the decision process is adequately defined, real-time management will become feasible, practical, and necessary.

PERT extends to the manager both an opportunity and a challenge. However, it must be useful at all levels; it must be understood, and it must be desired. This will take time and experience with modest programs before larger, integrated undertakings will be effective. In this way the dimensions of the new information technology may be better appreciated and planned for.

# THE VALUE OF PERT TO THE LINE MANAGER •

GABRIEL N. STILIAN

MANAGEMENT PLANNING and control methods have been on the scene for a long time, but they are now receiving attention from a number of managers who never before felt the need for such assistance in decision making. Among the various methods, they are turned more and more to PERT and such allied techniques as the critical path method and line of balance. These methods are gaining wide acceptance at all levels of management, for many applications, and in a variety of companies.

## PERT AND DECISION MAKING

One of the most important needs in business today is for systematic methods of assisting managers in making more accurate and precise decisions. They must have help in determining the correct course of action in their particular areas of responsibility. This aid will come from more meaningful information.

In order to operate at his greatest effectiveness, the manager must have at the proper time the accurate information necessary for decision making. Information is the external factor in decision making. The creative intelligence and practical experience of the decision maker are the internal factors which, when integrated with the necessary information, result in more precise decisions.

Because PERT is a systematic approach to developing information for decision making, it is making a very substantial contribution to the improvement of management. It is thereby helping to increase profits

GABRIEL N. STILIAN is Manager, Administrative Services Division, American Management Association, New York, New York.

because of the direct relationship between the profitability of a company and the decision-making ability of its managers.

PERT's contribution to profit has been enhanced by its ability to integrate decisions and activities which cut across corporate lines and which have not been properly unified and directed in the past. It has enabled managers with different responsibilities and backgrounds to understand problems and communicate ideas more effectively and to achieve the objectives of a program on an over-all rather than a segmented basis.

The complexity of modern business operations and the difficulty in making decisions in this environment have made inevitable the development of techniques which, like PERT, assist the manager in his difficult job. One observer of the business scene described the situation as follows:

> In managing the affairs of modern business and government, more scientific decision methods are needed. Unaided, the human mind cannot possibly weigh the manifold complexities involved in the development of a missile, the erection of a forty-story office building, the operation of an enterprise producing hundreds of products for millions of customers. Thousands of decisions go into scheduling jobs, ordering supplies, managing inventories, negotiating with contractors, hiring labor, pricing goods, and planning production facilities. The executive is further harassed by such uncertainties as the unpredictable tastes of consumers and the speculative nature of economic forecasts and research and development programs. Thus all too often he must act largely on hunch and intuition—and go home with the gnawing suspicion that he might have decided more wisely.

> In recent years scientists have been showing the executive how to avoid some of the perplexity that attends decision making. They have been putting together a voluminous bundle of mathematical techniques for evaluating possible courses of action. In attempting to rationalize the process of deciding, they have developed "decision theory." This is not really a single theory of how to make decisions, but rather a collection of techniques for weighing many factors in logical fashion. Some of the techniques are best suited to situations in which, though all the factors are known or predictable, the complexity is so confusing that the human mind cannot arrive at a wholly rational decision. Other techniques cope with "risks"—chances that can be accurately measured or calculated, such as the probability that a given number of insurance policy holders will die within a year. Still others deal with "uncertainties" (which scientists carefully distinguish from "risks")—chances that can be estimated only roughly at best, because, for example, they depend on future developments or the behavior of a competitor. All decision

theory, however, has a common purpose: to show decision makers surer ways to attain their goals.*

Managers are also beginning to discover that there are substantial advantages to be gained from *combining* some of the newer techniques such as operations research, data processing, systems planning, statistical analysis, PERT-type management information systems, and so forth. They are taking these new approaches and integrating them with management techniques that have proved their value in the past.

PERT AND PLANNING AND CONTROL

Unless the manager has some means of measuring the achievement of goals, he will not be able to evaluate the accuracy of his decision making. In other words, he needs some form of control information. But no control can be established unless he first develops a plan of action. Consequently, we see that in order to improve decision making, it is essential that there be precision in the planning and control aspects of the management job. Decisions must be based on plans and policies developed to meet objectives and must be related to control information which shows performance against plan.

PERT is particularly useful in planning and control activities. In work that has traditionally lacked definition, it is now possible with PERT to get results similar to those achieved in the planning and control of manufacturing activities. Although PERT techniques do not give the same absolute accuracy, there is reason to believe that they can provide advantages of equal or even greater importance to the profit of a company.

Because past management information systems have been inadequate, managers have been forced to make decisions based primarily on their own experience and the experience of other executives without the benefit of the necessary information. PERT has been welcomed by many managers as a help in making accurate forecasts, predicting problems, planning, scheduling, measuring work, and controlling results more effectively.

In developing a PERT information system for integrated management and decision making, the following steps must be taken:

1. Determining end objectives and goals.

* George A. W. Boehm, *Fortune*, April 1962, p. 128.

2. Establishing a plan based on these objectives.
3. Developing a forecast related to the plan.
4. Structuring in a systematic way activity and decision requirements.
5. Programing the manpower and other resources required.
6. Executing these activities according to the plan.
7. Devising measures for the control of the work.
8. Reporting and evaluating the results.
9. Appraising and reviewing the information for corrective action.
10. Developing preventive action and systems and for the improvement of plans based on the feedback of information.

Decisions are connected with planned actions and with the information feedback by means of the control system, which provides a comparison of results against the plan and shows progress and potential problems. Management information-system techniques will provide:

1. A means for determining objectives and defining problems.
2. Decision requirements for the profitable operation of a function.
3. Critical measures of performance which will be related to the requirements of the system.
4. Criteria upon which the decisions are properly based.
5. Information necessary for defining this criteria in a precise and timely fashion.
6. An information flow that ties together the activities and managers involved.

PERT alerts managers to the existence of a problem in advance. As a result, the information flow to decision centers can be structured in a more precise manner, and a PERT network can be drawn to integrate all the information requirements. This approach can be followed for practically any kind of management activity.

There are a number of questions which managers should ask themselves as they begin to consider the PERT technique. What is the reason for PERT's popularity? Is it permanent or passing? Has it proved to be profitable in actual use? What are its significant benefits? What are its problems and limitations? The ensuing chapters will answer these questions and deal with them in detail.

# SECTION II: PERT THEORY

*In order to understand how PERT can help him in his managerial duties, the line manager must know something of the basic technique on which PERT is based: network analysis. He will then have a frame of reference for those additional and original features which make up the fundamental principles of PERT. The manager should be aware of the fact that PERT was first applied to the control of the time element in business and that the next logical extension was to the cost factor.*

# THE BASIC TECHNIQUE: NETWORK ANALYSIS •

### E. T. ALSAKER

P ERT IS ONE FORM of the graphic network analysis technique. Network analysis was originally conceived for application to large programs, usually of a research and development nature. However, even where operations are on a smaller scale, network analysis can be used as a simple yet effective business technique. Essentially the network analysis technique consists of:

1. The development of a model (network) of some contemplated business activity or of one of its elements.
2. The evaluation of the network and adjustment of it in such a way as to provide a degree of assurance that, if the operating plan described by the network is followed, there will be a minimum of risk in reaching the objective on time and within the limits of acceptable cost.
3. The use of the network to monitor and control the operation it represents.

The network model is essentially a graphic, mathematical plan of action and provides an intelligible visual picture of the goals to be achieved and their interrelationships.

In other words, network analysis permits selection of the route by which we shall travel, together with some estimate of the hazards of the road prior to the time they are actually encountered. Management will certainly balance the hazards of the road (potential costs) on the one hand with the hazard of getting there late (missing schedule) on the other. Through network analysis, we will be able to choose the plan

E. T. ALSAKER is Manager of Management Systems Research, Lockheed-Georgia Company, Marietta, Georgia.

that offers the least total risk—that is, that strikes a balance between low cost with high schedule vulnerability and vice versa. The larger the operation on which a network is constructed, the less clearly can hazard relationships be demonstrated. But in the small enterprise, and in the small operation within the large enterprise, the relationships can be made very definite and clear.

THE NETWORK AS A COMMUNICATIONS DEVICE

If a man is going to write a book, he makes an outline before he starts. If he is going to analyze the financial status of a company, he puts figures down in some kind of accounting arrangement. If he is a systems analyst, he uses certain conventional forms to portray system flow and logic. Similarly, if he is going to make a plan for some future business operation, he should—among other things—prepare graphic charts, describe the plan in narrative detail, or construct an activity network.

The logic chart or flow diagram of the systems analyst is much more comprehensible than the same material in narrative form. More important, it enforces a certain discipline that will help to avoid gaps in the over-all logic of the system. A network produces a clear outline of the activities that must be undertaken and of the events that must occur before an end objective is reached. It provides a simple, clear, and readily understandable description of the business operation being undertaken.

Besides being a convenient shorthand for the planner, the network is an ideal communications medium. Even if it is a smaller one, the operation being planned will generally affect several groups, departments, and people. Without some easily understood physical picture of the whole plan, misunderstandings will often result. The various people involved will plan elements of what they think is an integrated whole but what is, in fact, fragmentary and disassociated. The advantage of having all concerned discuss and argue out details of relationships, inclusion of significant events, estimated times and the like—with a network plan before them while they are doing it—cannot be overemphasized. The clarity in a network leaves little room for confusion or doubt.

Equally important, the network communicates a picture of the whole plan to the managers of the business. Without such a plan, it is hard to find precise answers to such questions as: Why will this take so long?

Why can't this be done now? Why do you insist that the action you recommend is necessary? The manager, in thinking out the problem by himself, may not realize how and why his actions will affect some other manager or some other manager's may affect his. He may gauge the time required for an operation by the time that his people take in doing their part. It may not be clear to him that their work will be necessarily discontinuous and that they must at intervals wait on someone else.

With a network, however, the manager can get a firm grasp on the facts. He can see immediately why the job will take longer than he thought and that the schedule he has selected may have an adverse effect on workload and costs. He will be able to evaluate all the actions planned to see if they are necessary and why they are necessary. In brief, he no longer has a shaky set of opinions but now has a sound basis of facts on which he may proceed with confidence and dispatch.

The network can also be very useful in communicating the need for certain prescribed actions and schedules to people outside the company. Suppliers, customers, subcontractors, and others can get an over-all view of a program and act accordingly. It is certainly a familiar occurrence for a supplier or a subcontractor to diminish the importance of schedule compliance in regard to a service or product he is to provide. If the same subcontractor is made a party to the whole plan through the medium of a network, however, he will be able to see clearly the importance of his part and cooperate more effectively in making the operation a success. The network will assist the supplier in planning his own work and controlling his costs, when this type of coordination is desirable.

Familiar also is the complaint of customers or potential customers that schedules are too long. In the ordinary case, the manager probably does not have a much clearer grasp of why a particular schedule seems too long than the customer does; he just knows such and such a job always takes that long. In contrast, a network will often disclose ways of shortening the schedule. Whether it can be shortened or not, the network will at least give the manager a better idea of why it must be so long and will certainly make it easier for him to impress this knowledge on his customer.

Sometimes it is assumed that managers have a complete command of their plans and all the essential ramifications and do not need this kind of help at all; however, this is generally not the situation. In any case, the comparatively small amount of time spent in the preparation of a visual network plan will be adequately repaid by the value of the network as a communications device alone.

THE NETWORK AS A PLANNING INSTRUMENT

Regardless of its value as a communications device, a network's greatest value comes from its usefulness in the construction of a plan. When properly developed, a network is an admirable means of searching out all the intricacies and interrelationships of a projected operation —to whatever depth of detail is believed necessary for its proper management. In no other way can a plan be developed as efficiently and with as great assurance of its completeness.

Moreover, the completeness of the plan can be so clearly demonstrated to the project managers that they may proceed with it in full confidence that nothing important is left out. To assure this completeness, the planner must obviously give considerable thought to the limitations upon every event. He must make sure that all the significant ones are recognized and that the interrelationships will be, in fact, what he has depicted. The manager can review and appraise the value of the plan by thinking it out along the same lines followed by the planner, and with his wider knowledge he may find some limitations that are unknown to the planner. He may also find that certain policy matters intervene. The point is that planning is no longer a guessing game. The planner comes up with an objective presentation, and the manager is able to evaluate it in an orderly and effective manner. Together they will come up with superior results. Thus, time is saved and costs are reduced.

Since the completeness of the plan can be substantiated, the possibility of misunderstanding is lessened. We have all listened to alibis when something necessary to an operation has been left undone. A network can be of significant help in assuring that things that need to be done will be done and that alibis will be unnecessary. If this does not happen, both the planner and the manager may need more training in the use of network analysis techniques. With adequate care in the original construction of the plan and with careful observation of results in relation to the network as the plan proceeds, there should be no reason for important omissions.

Because network analysis is a planning and control tool, the network must be developed by (or in conjunction with) the person responsible for the actual operation, if it is to be of maximum usefulness. In most cases several departments will be involved in the planning and execution of a program. Network techniques allow subdivision of the work; each person may proceed with the detailed planning of his own part. A number of separate detailed networks can be put together quickly and simply to form a complete operating plan. In the process of putting them together, some adjustments for interdepartmental relationships will always have to be made. These can be worked out jointly by the respective departments. Networks for small operations are usually worked out in their entirety by a conference of those involved.

After the first network plan for a project has been constructed, the planners and managers must evaluate it to determine whether it is the best one or whether changes are warranted. The first plan represents a comprehensive scheme for the operation being undertaken. Even though the network may not yet include time estimates and even though the exact nature of some of the activities in it will not be known, it reliably presents the most essential facts concerning elements of the program. It is, therefore, a dependable basis for analysis and evaluation. Among the objectives of network development are the establishment of the shortest realistic time and the most economical means. Evaluation of the first network should proceed with these objectives in mind.

Alternative plans will ordinarily be found to be reasonable and worthy of further study. Some of these may show up in the development of the first network. Others may become obvious when the network is reviewed as a whole by project managers. Reasonable alternative approaches should be sketched, either as complete networks or as variances from the network already drawn.

As soon as all reasonable approaches to the physical performance of the task have been sketched out, activity times are inserted. Techniques used in obtaining reliable time estimates depend on the particular circumstances. Those responsible for performance of the actual activities should estimate times, but they need to be carefully checked by some other knowledgeable person. Records of past performance, suppliers' schedules, and so forth should be reviewed thoroughly. Any differences, of course, will be resolved with the person who made the original estimate.

The critical path and total activity time along the critical path are determined for each network. Although a computer may be used for this analysis, smaller networks should be analyzed manually or by using conventional office machines. The total time developed represents, for each operating plan, the probable elapsed time for the whole task. A direct time comparison of the various plans and of the extent of time risk inherent in each alternative is thereby made possible. At this point none of the plans with their associated estimated times may give promise of achieving successful schedule performance. If this is so, a review should be made to see if there is not some operating scheme that will reduce total time without unduly increasing cost or risk. These methods will help assure adoption of a plan that will satisfactorily achieve schedule. However, the plan will still not necessarily provide adequate cost performance. Further procedures are necessary to set and evaluate cost objectives.

When the several networks or, more likely, a single network with its variations has been constructed, it may be obvious that nothing worthwhile will be achieved by undertaking an evaluation of probable costs. If so, the choice of a plan will depend on time and time-risk considerations alone. On the other hand, particularly where added costs (overtime, premium costs, and so on) are necessary to speed up the operation sufficiently to meet the required completion schedule, cost estimating for alternative plans may be called for, and carefully estimated costs may be assigned to all activities on each network. Added or premium costs must be estimated for *all* activities having negative slack, and not just for those along the most critical path. If there are likely to be significant differences among the plans, costs of supplemental activities that are not shown on the networks should be added along with unallocated overhead.

In some cases, the network showing the least time will also show the least cost, and it will, of course, be automatically selected. If it does not, some management decision will be necessary. This decision will take into account the relative estimated costs evaluated against the increased possibility of missing schedule which is inherent in the longer-time as compared with the shortest-time network plan. Perhaps management will also take into account the relative risks inherent in the various times and choose the plan with least risk, provided other considerations are about equal.

Management may reconsider the need and economic desirability of the schedule selected. Confronted with the risks and costs involved, it may review the network plan and ask whether it would be advisable, for example, to defer installation of a machine for some months or perhaps not install it at all, to negotiate a new schedule with the customer— perhaps at a reduced price—or even to negotiate a price increase for a delivery schedule that is now known to be difficult and costly to meet. Network analysis is, if anything, a deterrent to setting unrealistic goals. If it comes into common use, preparation of a network may precede the setting of schedules and not be just a device to find out the best way to meet one that is already set.

THE NETWORK AS A CONTROL MECHANISM

It is clear that a network can be and should be used as a dynamic control mechanism. This will mean that the technique will have to be eminently practical, direct, and timely. We are referring here to control of work to assure that the end-event schedule will be met, although cost considerations are not ignored. Use of a network for such control assumes that there is a reliable method of reporting occurrences of events and also some means of knowing whether the next events to be completed will be reasonably within the time expected. For example, if an activity has a 12-week estimated span but at the end of the eighth week it is clear the activity will not be completed for about eight weeks more, adjustments in the network may have to be made immediately.

As the work progresses, the network will have to be kept up to date— week by week or day by day—if it is to continue its control function. Significant departures from estimated times, changes in the environment, or changes in policy may make revisions in the network desirable if it is to remain a practical and realistic control instrument.

The astute manager will keep an eye on even the remote events. If the operation is the installation of a computer, for instance, he will certainly watch the manufacturer's progress in producing a compiler needed to assemble programs that he is having written in a particular language. If the manufacturer's progress is less than promised, he will evaluate the effect on the plan as a whole and take whatever action is needed. If some other event shows signs of slippage, he will take action in the correct places and not just randomly. He will not have to panic or delay schedules if some suitable alternative exists; on the other hand, he may see that the probable costs of the alternative action are such as to warrant a forthright decision to delay the schedule, even though the delay may be considered unfortunate by company management. In any event, he will be able to state his case unequivocally. Many programs have been excessively costly because some manager had settled on an unrealistic plan or failed to follow what was a realistic plan or was caught completely unawares by some happening whose effect on the plan he did not foresee.

There is no reason why a network cannot be used as an aid in the control of costs. If such control is desired in those cases where it will be meaningful and beneficial, the cost-accounting system should be adapted to report costs of major activities in the network. In many cases this would not be much of a problem. Obviously, if control is to be forward-looking, cost reporting must be timely, since it is presumed that a historical cost collection would not of itself assist much in control —and this is likely to be more of a problem.

Before going ahead with such a control project, however, one should consider the consequences very closely and judge the potential benefits. Oddly enough, the shortcomings of the cost-control approach become more apparent on the larger projects. Some of the possible problems are as follows:

1.  It may be difficult to get good time estimates without giving oper-ating people the idea that budgets will be set at the same time. Just as time estimates should not become budgets, cost estimates should not become budgets either; but there is a strong tendency for them to do so. The validity of time estimates should, there-fore, not be prejudiced merely to get cost estimates.

2.  Actual cost accumulations may not be timely enough to be really useful. If a large and costly activity is measured only upon its completion, nothing much is gained in the way of control. It is usually difficult to determine the percentage completed for the activities in question; therefore, costs are usually evaluated only upon completion of the activities.

3.  It is not likely that costs can be truly optimized through manipu-lations on a computer. We often do not know enough about cost patterns and the way costs react in ordinary cases to make valid and realistic mathematical determinations that point the way to the least costs. There certainly are exceptions, particularly when

single, discrete, and simple cost situations are visualized. In a whole network, however, hardly any two costs will react alike.

4. Although it is usually easy to collect the costs of network activities, this is not always so. Unfortunately, it is sometimes impossible for various functions to concentrate on the same areas: engineering may deal with whole systems, for example, while manufacturing deals with major assemblies.

5. Certain costs cannot be assigned to specific activities, and these costs are frequently substantial. To the extent that arbitrary prorations must be used, these costs for the control purpose at hand become meaningless.

In spite of these difficulties, it is clear that some networks can be of real advantage as devices for cost control. When time estimates are obtained, for instance, it is frequently necessary to clarify the basis on which they are made—such as crew sizes or hours per week. Whatever the basis, they can be helpful in making or analyzing cost estimates. Furthermore, in some cases where no standard hours or detailed estimates or any of the familiar measures are established, relating actual activity costs to estimates may be the best means available. It will therefore pay to be on the alert for opportunities for cost control.

Regardless of whether a network is to be used for cost-control purposes, it may be desirable to estimate the costs of alternative plans, however informally this may be done. If the network is to be used for control, the estimates of important activities in the network must be assigned on a somewhat more formal basis so that they will serve as targets for cost performance. For most business applications, there is no need to estimate costs on a multiple basis: that is, *optimistic, most likely, pessimistic.* There is no probable distribution of costs that can be used to construct a normal distribution curve such as the one the PERT technique uses for time estimates. The best approach will generally be to estimate a probable single cost for the activity. Careful selection of operating plans and judicious choices among alternatives in reallocating resources may lead to courses of action that one would hope to be least costly for the enterprise as a whole.

From a practical standpoint, even the most flexible of accounting systems will not be able to measure all network activities equally well. However, if the cost of a particular activity is important to management, it will be helpful to make a comparison between activity costs estimated and reported costs to the extent it is economically feasible to do so. Management may wish to follow the cost of only one or a few important activities. These can be followed independently of the others, and if poor cost performance is to be especially guarded against, perhaps some of the activities should be further subdivided so that costs may be measured in greater detail.

The advantage of using a network rather than some independent set of subdivisions to control costs is that the network will presumably be used for schedule and performance control as well. When an event occurs, some activity or activities have been completed; the cost system at that point can measure the actual cost of the activities against the previous estimates and assist management in determining whether cost performance to date is satisfactory or whether it must be improved on subsequent activities if cost and profit objectives are to be met. The following are some of the benefits of relating both estimated and actual costs to network activities:

1. Review of actual costs incurred in relation to estimated costs will tend to disclose work inputs that are badly calculated to meet the required estimated times. If little cost is incurred, it is a fair assumption that a minor amount of work has been completed. Conversely, the review may disclose work inputs in excess of those required and unwarranted overtime that is likely to exceed estimated costs.

2. Costs are broken down into more manageable increments. It will be possible to detect elements out of control and take remedial action at a very early date.

3. It will be easier to estimate manpower, costs, cash flow, and so forth by time intervals.

The network and its associated activity times represent, in a sense, a quantitative model of the project to be analyzed. Estimated costs are a logical addition to that model. At the time that elements of the model are compared with actual performance, activities and their associated costs may be considered. In cases where such control is desired and where it will be meaningful and valuable, relationships of time and cost will be clarified, and the management of both may be improved.

In those cases where networks are not used formally as an instrument of cost control, the project manager must retain an awareness of cost as work under the plan proceeds. Few complex plans will prove out exactly as originally expected from first to last; unanticipated difficulties and other factors will necessitate changes in the plan if schedule is to be met. Whenever a significant change has to be made, the effect on estimated costs must be evaluated to see whether the project will still stay within acceptable cost bounds. If not, other courses of action must be sought.

There is a secondary use of the network. By placing names on each activity, it has been possible for companies to pinpoint responsibility and also assure that a person is not expected at any one time to carry an impossible lead. By budgeting people's time in this way, it is possible to reassign responsibilities or change the plan to reduce duplications.

WHEN TO USE A NETWORK

Network analysis is used to best effect in connection with (1) the new and untried, (2) the infrequently repeated operation, and (3) the operation on which schedule and cost controls are critical. Established operations that are routine, repetitive, and performed frequently are poor candidates for use of network analysis techniques. In such cases, process charting might better be used to control efficiency. For example, a publisher would not use network analysis to get daily newspapers out on time. On the other hand, he might very well use it in changing over to a major new system, whatever that system might be.

No hard-and-fast rules can be given. Depending on circumstances, the extent of application will vary from a simple, hand-sketched network without times or costs to an elaborate system of multilevel networks analyzed by a computer and accompanied by detailed cost estimates and cost reporting. Needless to say, the cost of each should be justified by the benefits to be gained.

Network analysis need not be confined to the first unit made in a production series. It might be useful on the first ten but not on the hundredth. It may be applied at an interval of an operation—for example, in planning and controlling a major change in design of a product already in production. It may be used to control a model change, a departmental rearrangement, installation of new equipment, the remodeling of a building, the introduction of new systems and procedures, or all of the many smaller non-routine tasks that must be occasionally performed.

Exhibit 1 concerns the planned installation of equipment for data

EXHIBIT 1:

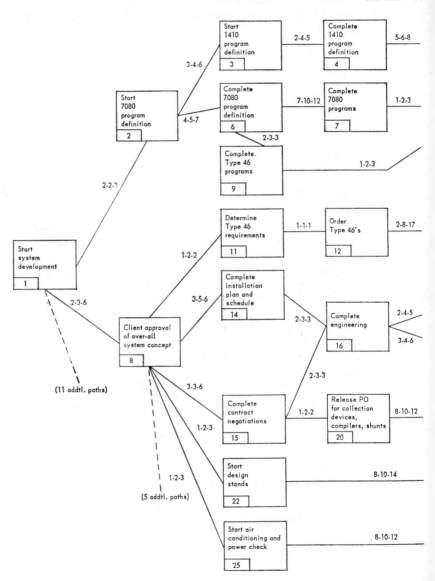

## INSTALLATION OF A DATA COLLECTION SYSTEM

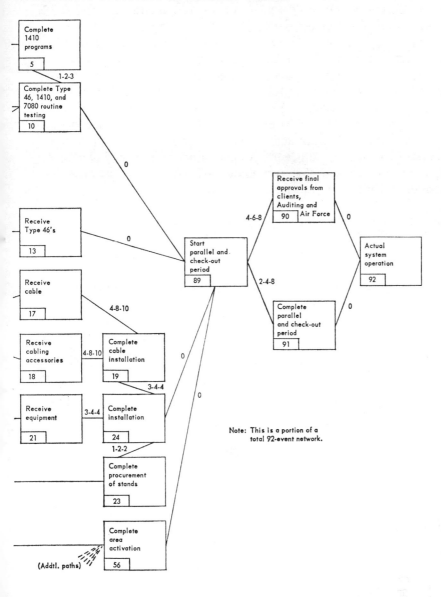

Note: This is a portion of a
total 92-event network.

collection and transmission in shop areas. This equipment was designed to record employee attendance, labor charges, shop-order movements, material disbursements, measures taken for quality assurance, and the like—using prepunched cards, punched employee badges, and variable dials—and to transmit the data by wire to a central location. This project affected a large number of people, departments, and related systems. Equipment had to be selected and procured, stands and other related property designed and built, card forms designed and ordered, systems developed, programs written, people trained in both the use of the equipment and the handling of its products, and many other miscellaneous tasks performed. Network analysis made it possible to get all these steps in proper sequence and perspective and provided a method of continuing follow-up to assure that everything required to make the installation successful was done on time.

### ESTABLISHING A NETWORK ANALYSIS PROGRAM

The network analysis is a simple and straightforward technique which produces such significant benefits that it tends to be readily accepted. Nevertheless, there are certain fundamentals that contribute to the overall value of the program which must be thoroughly grasped.

Network analysis is a tool for use by the people responsible for planning and controlling activities. It is their function and their responsibility and not that of a centralized planning staff: they must participate in the program. If someone else handles it for them, the plans will tend to be much less effective. In organizing a network analysis program, this important factor must be one of the basic considerations. The extent to which organization should be formalized will depend on the particular case.

First of all, it would be wise for the company to select representatives of major activities such as manufacturing, engineering, administration, sales, and finance to form a group for over-all policy formulation. These representatives should report through their major organization heads to top management. It should be their responsibility to see that all steps necessary to encourage the use of network analysis and train people in its use are taken. A company manual and training program may be required. The policy group should have definite authority and responsibility to see that these are provided and that some formal or informal organization to deal with problems exists. They will normally assist with the organization and application of the technique within their respective functional areas and will be primarily responsible for selling the program, if that is required.

It is desirable to have working representatives (possibly full-time) from the departments most concerned with projects for which networks are constructed. These people act as liaison between the line functions and the central group. They interview people in their organizations in developing network plans, obtain time estimates, follow up on event occurrences and activity completions, and generally take responsibility for the segments of the network charged to the organizations they represent. They deal with similar representatives from other organizations in working out common problems, resolving points of organizational conflict, and assuring the development of compatible schedules (obviously a chain of activities that contains considerable positive slack for one organization alone may be on the critical or near-critical path for some other). Finally, because a large program involves considerable clerical, drafting, and similar detail, enough service people connected with the central staff should be available to carry on these activities.

To make this organization effective, top management should issue a clear statement of objectives and responsibilities. This authorization should cite the basic objectives of the program and the things management expects to be done, and it should establish the policy group and see it well on the way toward the successful performance of its duties. This policy group is of major importance in making the network analysis program truly effective and beneficial to the company.

Top management should so express its interest directly to middle managers as to assure that they will adopt network analysis as an operating tool for use in their everyday functions. The policy group and its representatives will have the responsibility of assisting these managers with organizational matters within their areas. Middle managers, in turn, should support and develop network analysis among first-line managers. Operating managers should be visited personally, and someone should explain the program, answer their questions, and assist them in using this technique in their operations. The success of the program will finally depend on the cooperation of these managers, and no effort should be spared in enlisting their support.

True enthusiasm for network analysis will usually result from actual experience in using it on a line problem. This problem should be one of sufficient consequence. It is important that the technique be emphasized as a simple, down-to-earth management tool useful at all levels of management. It should not be overglamorized or peddled as a panacea, which it is not. Unless the networks need to be formalized for some good purpose (such as preparing an exhibit for proposal to management), they should be left in their crude working state. They will need to be changed often anyway, and as long as a readable reproduction can be made from them, their purpose will be served. Means should be minimized and results stressed; the network must convey a message and should never be made too elaborate.

Finally, the network analysis program should be interwoven with the company's general management information and control system. Its results should be included in project reporting. Reports of network analyses to management should not be duplicated by other non-integrated reports of the same data. Uncoordinated, badly organized reports are a poor testimonial to a technique that is supposed to be an effective tool of operating management. The added effort required to translate reports into conventional forms can cause extra expense and reporting delays. Certain general considerations should be taken into account:

1. Reports should indicate clearly that they arise from analyses of activity networks.
2. Unwarranted translation into forms other than those customarily used for such activities as critical- and slack-path analyses, on the grounds that the latter would not be understood by management, should be thoroughly questioned. These reports may be intelligible to all management levels after brief explanation.
3. The extent of detail reported should be appropriate to the manager to whom the report is directed. Ordinarily, this can be easily handled by creating the network in suitable levels.
4. If costs of activities on the network are reported, it is advisable to combine schedule and cost data in the same report. This should include sufficient data on the relationships between estimated and actual costs to indicate to the manager the likelihood that costs will be under or over those anticipated.
5. The report on costs should be in such form that *all* costs, and not just those associated with network activities, are included. There should be assurance that reported costs accurately reflect transac-

tions on the company's books. This seems an elementary admonition, but unfortunately there have been instances in which it might better have been heeded.

6. Reports for operating managers should not contain data that can be understood only by a statistician. Unexplained variance computations often fall in this category.

7. Reports should not only indicate clearly what the current status is but also show either that there are no conditions requiring action or that action is being taken to remedy unsatisfactory conditions. All explanations should be brief.

## TECHNICALITIES OF NETWORK ANALYSIS

It is always difficult to produce order from disorder. The network planner can simplify his task and get better results if he follows certain simple rules. The following series of steps will fit the average case:

1. Define the end objective precisely. This is frequently difficult, but close definition is fundamental to a complete plan.

```
┌─────────────────────┐
│      EVENT A        │
│                     │
│   COMPLETION OF     │
│   NETWORK END       │
│    OBJECTIVE        │
└─────────────────────┘
```

2. Define all significant events that are precedent to the end objective. Do not start on any "chain" until this is done. The purpose is, of course, to make sure that no elements are left out inadvertently.

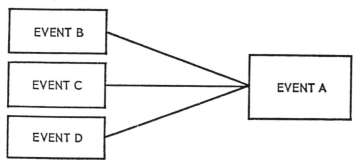

3. Define all significant events precedent to Event *B*. This is a continuation of the strategy in the second step. Again, the purpose is to assure that nothing significant in the whole plan is left out.

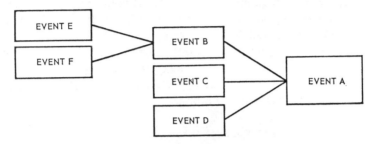

4. Define all significant events precedent to Event *C*. If it is found that some event already shown is precedent to the event being worked on, interconnecting lines must be drawn (see asterisks).

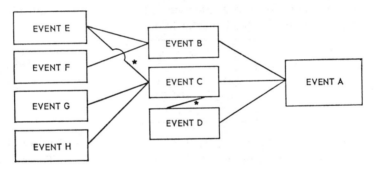

5. Continue in a similar manner with other events. Work back a level at a time, making sure that all significant precedent events are established.

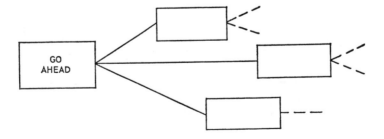

6. Make sure that all events except the beginning and ending ones have at least one connection on each end. Recheck for any important events left out. If there are any, there has been a serious error somewhere. If the omitted event is really important, find out whether it is covered by the scope of the work or related to it.

In developing the network, it is important to discard irrelevant matters from consideration. There is a tendency to include events that the planner considers necessary, even though they are not essential to the end objective as it has been defined. Although these events may be written down somewhere for reference and follow-up, they should be kept out of the network.

Since it will be convenient most of the time to have the organizations responsible for the various elements of the whole task prepare the network portions applicable to their own specialties, a problem may arise in controlling the work sufficiently to insure a reliable result. It is useful in some cases at least to farm out portions of a top-level network. A simple example is shown in Exhibit 2. Activities which might be farmed out are *A* and *G* to manufacturing; *C, D,* and *E* to engineering; *B* to quality control; and *F* to shipping. Each would then produce a network for the activities concerned, with the same beginning and end events as on the main network. The whole network can then be woven together (including any organizational points of conflict that may not have shown up on the main network).

Some managers may want to keep more detailed control over activities to avoid undisclosed potentials for exceeding budgeted costs and missing

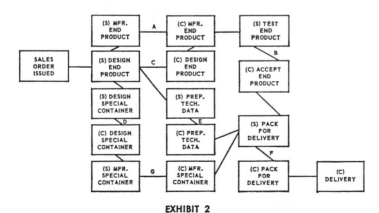

**EXHIBIT 2**

schedules. They may want to know, week by week, what percentage of work is finished as well as what costs are incurred. A few companies have accounting systems that will allow this, but most do not.

A word of caution on the use of percentages: It is essential that system controls be such as to avoid misleading figures. For example, suppose that an activity has an applied 1,000 standard hours and management wants to measure standard hours completed week by week. At the end of some interval, 500 hours' worth of work, say, may have been reported as completed. Now suppose that the following week an additional 100 hours' worth is completed but that 300 hours' worth of work previously finished is rejected because it was spoiled in a subsequent operation. A poorly designed system might show that 60 per cent (500 + 100 = 600, or 60 per cent of 1,000) of the activity is finished. Actually, only half that much is now done at most. It might be even less of a disproportionately large number of parts will be required to get an acceptable final unit of production.

A better way to measure performance of the activity would be to break it down on a subnetwork into smaller increments with events whose completion can be individually determined. "Start assembly *A*" and "Complete assembly *A*" can be broken down as shown in Exhibit 3.

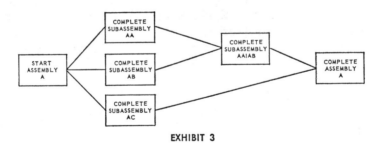

**EXHIBIT 3**

An interesting problem arises when it is known that the operating plan will be something less than ideal (see Exhibit 4*A*). If the assembly is an aircraft substructure, for instance, we would know that this relationship, while possibly desirable, is impractical. We would also know that some purchased part may be installed when the assembly is well advanced and that it need not be available before work begins. On an upper-level network the relationships may be represented as shown in Exhibit 4*B*. However, for closer control, the situation might be shown in more detail on a lower-level network as is shown in Exhibit 4C.

The orderly administration of a program using network analysis presupposes careful definition of events. "Complete the design" can mean six different things to six different people. Any communications scheme with this degree of indefiniteness can quickly become intolerable. As a practical matter, the network events have a reasonably definite meaning to those who deal with them every day. On any but a very small scale, however, misunderstandings will occur even within the inner group, to say nothing of those outside this group.

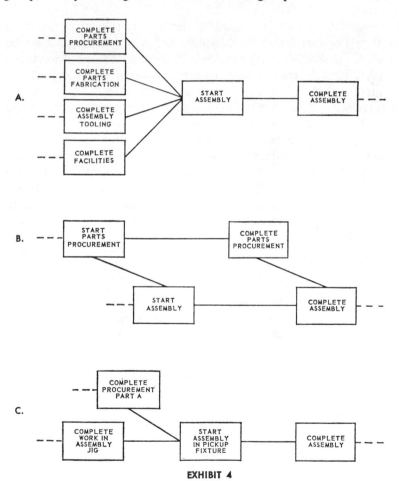

EXHIBIT 4

It is advisable, therefore, to define events in writing. When it is practical, definitions ought to contain the following:
1. Abbreviations used.
2. The long form of the abbreviated terms.
3. An exact definition of the event.
4. The specific indication or evidence that the event has occurred.
5. The organization responsible for reporting occurrence.

If the same events are included in several networks, the definitions should be standard ones: that is, "complete the design" should have the same meaning in all networks.

The occurrence of events should be signaled by substantial evidence other than the completion of activities, and this evidence should be included in the definitions. For example, the event "(S) pack for delivery" in Exhibit 2 depends on three others: "(C) mfr. special container," "(C) prep. tech data," and "(C) accept and product." To affirm that these three are completed is not evidence of the occurrence of the event "(S) pack for delivery." This point can become very important. For general applications, network analysis is always event-oriented.

Activities on a network will have to be named or described—that is, we must pay attention to not only the nature of events but also the nature of connecting activities. Defining these activities can result in a useful inquiry into the elements of the plan. Consider the example in Exhibit 5. What is the nature of activity *A?* It can be correctly deduced as the installation in the assembly of the last part to be received, and the time ascribed would then be the time for this assembly. Therefore, improbable as it may have seemed at the outset, the activity may be described as "install GTC unit."

In general applications, however, it is desirable to ignore the nature of activities in the initial construction of the network. When we explore into activities, we will probably find it necessary to insert a few more event points to take account of, say, changes of responsibility. If "(C)

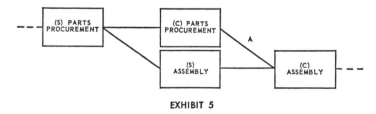

EXHIBIT 5

Assembly" involves final inspection, it might be improper to include inspection in the *A* activity; if so, an additional event point will be needed. All of this offers no particular difficulty and is definitely helpful in thinking out the plan.

Whether single "most likely" times, or sets of "optimistic, most likely, and pessimistic" times should be assigned to activities will be determined by circumstances. In some cases a single time for an activity will be most appropriate: the likelihood of deviation is not substantial. There may be no deviation because management will take whatever steps are necessary to maintain schedule. (This is not a wholly valid argument because management might seek information on the *extent* of the risk to schedule.) In any event, if a computer is not needed or available, it will simplify things if single times are used.

Where a program is on less solid ground and where probabilities are less sharply limited, sets of times may be preferable. If we remember that the estimated time is usually calculated from the set of times, using a formula that is based on a premise reasonably suitable in most but not necessarily all instances, it may be found advisable to modify the formula in particular cases to get a better approximation of reality. This will depend upon the circumstances and no fixed rule is needed.

We should be conscious of the probabilities and risks inherent in a plan. The concept of a "most likely time" as "*n* weeks, give or take something" (the standard deviation) is a useful one. So is the concept of probability as traditionally determined and expressed as some factor that can be interpreted as so many chances out of a hundred. Somewhat more obscure but equally useful is the concept of variance. It has been rightfully said that time can be bought with money or risk; if we lack a variance figure, however, the *extent* of risk is not apparent. In accepting added risk, we increase probability. If we ignore variance, how can we demonstrate increased risk? The manager may know intuitively that it is there but be wholly unfamiliar with its extent. The risk can be correctly evaluated as the relative increase in the variance figure. ("Variance" for this purpose is interpreted as "the square root of the sum of the squares of the *b–a* ranges of activities on the critical path after the sum is divided by 36.") Experience teaches that the risks inherent in some of the activities involved in general industrial applications are extreme. Ignoring the extent of relative risks involved in alternative plans can be a shortsighted practice.

Consistency in estimating activity times is also important. These are the times used by normal workforces working a normal workweek. It is a good idea in many instances to record the number of people, man-hours, machines times, and so on as documentation for the estimates and for later reference. The estimates should be made without regard to any schedule considerations.

A principal purpose of network analysis is to permit management to apply resources to a task only to the extent required to meet schedule. If a network is constructed using normal times throughout, the correct extent to which resources should be reapplied and overtime worked will be evident. If, however, the network times have been estimated with the required schedule in mind and in an attempt to fit it, two things will happen: (1) the planner will mistakenly overestimate the resources required for some activities, and (2) he will lose track of some of his manipulations and show applications or reapplications of resources other than where they should be. Both results will increase costs and diminish the effectiveness of management. On the contrary, if a network is constructed using estimated normal times, those activities requiring no overtime or extra application of effort will be immediately apparent. Overtime or extra effort for activities with negative slack can be planned to the extent required and no more.

If a network using normal times comes up with negative slack, one of two things can be done. Preferably, the network should be left alone (if the operating plan is unchanged) so that extra resources required can be highlighted during the life of the project. This will make it necessary for operating supervisors to keep management informed of what is being done to stay on schedule—that is, to pick up the negative slack. However, the network activity times may be adjusted to remove negative slack on the various paths. A careful record should be kept of the estimated overtime or extra effort required to accomplish this, and a summary should be prepared for the program manager.

# FUNDAMENTAL PRINCIPLES AND APPLICATIONS OF PERT •

ERNEST O. CODIER

P ERT IS A SYMBOL used to represent a set of concepts. These concepts include: (1) network representation of plans; (2) prediction of time schedules; (3) recognition and measurement of uncertainty; and (4) adaptability to environment and circumstances. These ideas taken together form the basis for a constructive technique designed to help with the management job, regardless of the industry a manager may be in.

ELEMENTS OF PERT

The following are the elements on which these PERT concepts are built:

1. *An event.* This is an inexplicitly identifiable point in time at which something has happened or a situation has come into existence. There may be work involved in approaching an event, but the event itself takes no time, and therefore no work is represented by an event.

2. *An activity.* This is a clearly definable task to which a known quantity of manpower and other resources will be applied. In basic PERT, an activity represents effort applied over a period of time and is bounded by two events. These events are referred to as the predecessor and successor events for the associated activity.

3. *Time estimates.* PERT associates an elapsed time with an activity.

ERNEST O. CODIER is Manager, Engineering Resources Planning and Analysis, Light Military Electronics Department, Defense Electronics Division, General Electric Company, Utica, New York.

In order to determine in advance what this time is likely to be, it is necessary to estimate. The estimating procedure is the cornerstone of the PERT technique: someone who is capable of actually performing the activity in question is asked for *three* time estimates:

    *a.* An *optimistic* time: the time which would be required if everything worked out or proceeded ideally. This is an unrealistic estimate to the extent that it can be expected to occur in approximately only one case out of 100.

    *b.* A *pessimistic* time: this is the opposite of the optimistic estimate. Barring totally uncontrollable situations such as fires and floods, it tells us what time would be required if everything which could logically go wrong *does* go wrong. This estimate is also unrealistic, representing the worst case of one out of a hundred.

    *c.* A *most likely* time: the time which, in terms of the estimator's past experience, this activity is most likely to take in the circumstances expected to exist.

4. *Expected time.* The three time estimates are combined mathematically in two formulas which produce two items of information. The first is the PERT expected time—that is, the time that divides the total range of probability in half. There is a 50-50 chance that the time actually required will be equal to or greater than the expected time.

5. *Spread.* Another manipulation provides a measure of the degree of uncertainty associated with the expected time. This measure tells us the width or spread of the center 50 per cent of the total distribution so that we can say that there is a 50-per-cent probability that this activity will take the expected time—plus or minus so many weeks.

6. *Network.* In doing a job, our first step is to analyze the component tasks and their interdependencies. The result of this analysis is a network of events and interconnecting activities that defines the series and parallel sequences of activities and events which must occur to achieve the end objective. The second step in doing a job is to secure time estimates and calculate the expected time for each activity. We can then determine the probable length of time required for the various series-sequences of

activities which connect the start of the program with the objective event.

7. *Critical path.* One of these sequences will be longer than all the rest; this longest path is called the critical path because it is the one which determines the length of time required to reach the objective event. It has two principal features. First, if the program is to be shortened, one or more of the activities on this longest path must be shortened or eliminated. The application of additional effort anywhere else in the network will be useless unless the critical path is shortened first. Second, if the time required for the actual performance of an activity on the critical path varies from the calculated expected time, this variation will be reflected in a one-to-one fashion in the anticipated accomplishment of the objective event—no matter how far in the future that event may be.

8. *Slack.* Since the critical path is defined as the longest path in time from the starting event to the objective event, then all other events and activities in the network must lie on paths which are shorter. That means that along these paths there is slack, or time to spare. These paths are referred to as slack paths and are the areas where surplus resources of men, facilities, or time are to be found.

In order to measure the amount of slack existing in any point in the network, we must determine the earliest expected time and the latest allowable time for each event. The *earliest expected time* for an event is defined as the sum of the expected times for the activities along the longest path leading from the starting event up to the event in question. The *latest allowable time* is determined by adding the expected times for activities on the longest path leading *back* from the objective event to the event in question and by subtracting this sum from the schedule date for the objective event. The latest allowable time is that time by which an event must occur if slippage of the objective event schedule is to be avoided.

Slack, then, is the difference between the earliest expected and latest allowable times. It represents flexibility. A *range* of time over which the activity can take place without influencing the accomplishment of the objective. Slack areas have not only spare time but also surplus resources of men and facilities.

9. *Probability of success.* A simple arithmetic calculation on the three time estimates enables us to obtain a measure of the uncertainty of the expected time for the activity. Since the expected time for any event is calculated by adding up expected activity— the various times on the longest path leading to that event—we can also statistically combine the uncertainties involved in each activity in such a way as to obtain a measure of the uncertainty in the expected time for the event. Thus, when we calculate the PERT expected time for the end event of a program, we can also obtain a measure of the *uncertainty* or the range of probable error in our prediction. By another mathematical procedure we may compare the PERT predicted expected time and its uncertainty with the schedule commitment for the objective event and derive the probability of meeting the schedule.

### THE CAPABILITIES OF PERT

The use of the basic PERT device provides a number of capabilities. PERT makes it possible for us to:
1. Plan in advance the action which must be taken to produce a desired result in the future.
2. Predict the probable performance time required by our plan.
3. Improve the plan, when we find that the predicted performance is not good enough.
4. Measure performance against the plan, after the plan is set in motion.
5. Control progress by using information and visibility provided to initiate timely and economical replanning actions.

In order to implement PERT at all, we are required at the outset to think through and get down on paper the proposed plan of action for the program. The plan rendered visible for analysis purposes is rendered equally visible for troubleshooting purposes and the correction of errors. It should not be necessary to belabor the value of this step of reducing the detailed plan to a written document; it is a valuable discipline which simply codifies what we have been doing all along and enforces thorough planning.

PERT provides the ability to predict times to completion for any event in the network. We have seen many management control techniques come and go which did no more than tell us what we already knew. The ability of PERT to predict times and uncertainties of performance in the future is one of the ways in which it gives us information that we did not already have.

We can evaluate our plan before we start. If the predicted results do not satisfy the required objectives, we can revise the plan before we reach the point of no return. We can revise it while we still have *time* to recover. We can save money by eliminating things which we normally do but for which we don't have *time* in particular instances.

Any device which can predict can be used for measurement. As the program proceeds, we may substitute actual completion times for the original time estimates. Using this known data in combination with the times estimates for activities which have not yet occurred, we may continuously predict the time to completion for the major objectives.

When a program is under operational control, PERT will pinpoint the problem areas. If the predicted time to accomplishment of a major objective shows that the program has a low probability of accomplishing an assigned schedule, PERT directs attention to those relatively few activities which are creating the problem. In years past, when a program was in trouble, it was assumed that the *entire* program was in trouble, and most often everyone on the project was put on overtime. PERT now clearly shows that close to 90 per cent of this crash effort was wasted, since it was applied to activities which were on slack paths where there was already time to spare. PERT spells out the critical path as the area vital to the correction of predicted schedule difficulties. To help us concentrate on the critical path, the slack relationships in other portions of the network gives us information about manpower and facilities not fully utilized. Furthermore, knowledge of the interrelationships with other events or paths adjacent to the critical path enables us to avoid creating new problems while we are fixing the old ones.

METHODOLOGY FOR THE EFFECTIVE USE OF PERT

A tool must be applied with a *method*. The specifications for a method of application depend upon the nature of the tool, the environment within which it is to be used, and the kind of results desired. But underlying the specifications of method there must be an attitude of approach—a philosophy, if you will—which governs the methods. It will be this underlying philosophy which will make or break the success of any management system. The effective use of PERT involves the basics of PERT plus a methodology and whatever PERT extensions we may find useful in a particular company. None of the extensions of PERT capabilities will be of any use if our methodology does not create a situation wherein the basic device will be accepted and used. When PERT is properly presented and operated, the individual contributor finds that it takes his everyday problems into account and is responsive to all the requirements of planning at his level. The net result in our plant is that at the working levels of our projects, PERT program planning has enthusiastic acceptance.

If PERT does no more than provide our operating people with an effective tool for the improvement of their performance, it will be well worth the effort we put into it. Moreover, once a PERT plan has been formulated, a well-organized and visible plan exists which can be used for management purposes. We can improve the quality of our quotations—in terms of both price and delivery. We can have these quotations backed up with a detailed plan of how to go about making good on our promises. PERT can turn a contract from a management risk decision into a simple problem in technical planning.

This knowledge is sufficient to make any good manager strain at the leash, but this is the trap which can make PERT worse than useless. We still have with us the manager who spells control with a capital *C* and applies it under the mistaken impression that the evils of system can be cured with more system and that rigidity and review in great detail are the great panacea. In the hands of this type of man, PERT becomes just another damaging tool that hurts rather than helps company operations.

The various factors of human relationships in our work are not new, but they have assumed a new importance and significance in today's technology. These factors apply not only between the manager and his individual contributors but also between companies and their customers and suppliers. PERT provides the *capability* for a new effectiveness for program management, but it will not of itself assure that the change will occur. Neither PERT nor anything else can substitute for intelligent professional behavior. The potency of PERT as a device for pointless administrative snooping is unparalleled, and we must powerfully resist the temptation to use it for this purpose. We should use it to get the job done—but for nothing which does not directly contribute to getting the job done. If we are not careful and realistic about our relationships, PERT will become a very costly but impotent nuisance and we will see a valuable concept go down the drain.

## A PRACTICAL APPLICATION OF PERT

When PERT was announced to the public by the Navy, we did not have a contractual requirement for the use of PERT on any of our programs, but we were thoroughly aware of the problem of technical management in today's complex and changing technology. We investigated PERT and discovered that there were some key elements in it that could be of powerful assistance in handling our own management problems.

We also felt that its utility to us could be greatly enhanced by adopting a philosophy and an approach which were somewhat different from the Navy's original method of application. Any management system which is constructively and resourcefully used in a local environment must take on variations and be adapted to the particular company in which it is used. This is a fact not only to be recognized but also to be encouraged, since any tool must be so shaped and designed. However, it is important that variations should not be made unnecessarily—as has often been the case with PERT.

As the name implies, PERT was originally conceived as an after-the-fact evaluation or review of the effectiveness of a program plan. In its original use by the Navy it was just that: a device for progress and status review superimposed upon a program for the use of the highest level of program management. Viewed without the bias necessarily introduced by the. Navy's situation, it seemed to us at General Electric that a more general definition for PERT would be: *an analytical procedure for predicting performance time and evaluating uncertainty in program plans.*

Viewed in this way it seemed to us equally evident that PERT can also be used not only for planning but also for the measurement and improvement of planning. Furthermore, it is my conviction that PERT can be used as a basis for a new and vital approach to program management. Whether viewed from the standpoint of management control or as a planning tool for the individual contributor, PERT is outstandingly unique in that it recognizes and measures uncertainty.

In our method of operation, the group that is technically responsible for the accomplishment of the work gets together with one of our program planners. This man acts as a combination leader and devil's advocate. The objective in this group is to generate an initial plan for the program—to be done in the conservative and risk-free way that we would prefer. Thus, the first plan should be one in which there is essentially no technical risk. When this network plan is complete and shows all of the required activities, then and only then are the time estimates applied.

When obtaining the three time estimates, we ask first for the optimistic estimate and then for the pessimistic. The engineer has to stop and identify all those factors which have to go right for the optimistic estimate and assume that they will go wrong. This gives us the extremes, and we have the situation bracketed. Within the extreme range, he now selects the time, all things considered, that this task is most likely to take, and that is the third estimate. At this point, we have a *good* time estimate, plus some information we never had before—a measure of the uncertainty involved.

The way in which the three times are distributed is very revealing and helps to identify the nature of our problems. Consider the three distributions: 2-4-18, 5-6-7, 1-7-7—all are quite different but they all have a statistical expected time of six weeks. Under the old system of asking for one estimate, in each of the three cases we would have gotten an estimate of about seven weeks, and yet they *are* all different. Each one tells a significant story even before we resort to mathematics.

When all the time estimates are in, then the time analysis is performed either by hand or with a computer, depending upon the needs of the situation. The no-risk program plans arrived at by this procedure are clear and complete pictures of the project in which all foreseeable risk situations have been considered and covered. In today's market, however, a no-risk program is invariably too long. The time usually has to be shortened.

We use three basic methods to reduce program length. First, we may eliminate certain portions of the work. For example, in a computer job we may elect to go direct from logic diagrams to prototype hardware and eliminate the breadboard construction and testing cycle. This kind of decision involves additional risks. It is in this phase that archaic paperwork or anything else not absolutely necessary is eliminated.

The second method is to put into parallel those activities which normally would occur in series. For example, we would normally not start preparing the detail drawings for a piece of equipment until after the design has been frozen; therefore, we would not start the detail drawings until after the environmental testing was complete. However, we may shorten this cycle by working on the detail drawings simultaneously with the environmental testing. This sort of decision costs money: some of the drawings may have to be revised because of changes dictated by the environmental test results.

The third method is the application of additional resources—manpower, facilities, or the use of overtime effort. This is the most expensive method of all. And we prefer to hold overtime effort in reserve to help with any problems that may come up in the late stages of the program where this is the last resort. In any event, the PERT picture enables us to apply this costly method only at the points where it will be the most effective.

This, then, is the process of arriving at the initial operating plan, which represents our best knowledge at the beginning. But, as the program proceeds, we learn more about it, and we continually replan according to this increased knowledge. The program plan is never frozen, except for its end objectives.

When a program is under way and there is a slippage of predicted performance, the program planner goes first to the individual who is technically responsible and who points out the source of the difficulty and makes recommendations. His recommendations are incorporated in the network and immediately analyzed in order to evaluate their effect. In other words, the man responsible is given an opportunity to do his proper job, after which the PERT planner reviews the proposed changes and problems with higher management. Thus the manager is presented with completed staff work—the picture of a problem situation, the actions required to alleviate the problem, and the predicted results of these actions.

On the other hand, analysis of the problem may show that the man responsible has extended his authority to its limits and is still unable to cure the problem; he may need additional resources or action in another functional area; or his technical judgment may indicate that a more economical solution is available in an area outside of his cognizance. In cases of this type, action by his manager is called for, and this will be clearly demonstrable with the aid of the PERT network picture. For the first time we now have a management control technique that allows the responsible individual to communicate with his manager in a more precise and exact manner concerning the planning and control of his work.

## GUIDELINES FOR PERT APPLICATION

In the first place, we must recognize that a real commitment can exist only when there is a specific penalty which will be imposed for non-performance and that it operates to a man's ultimate disadvantage to pretend that there are commitments anywhere else. The only real commitments in our plant are the promises to the customer.

Second, we must remember that a time estimate is not a commitment. An estimate is the means by which subordinates inform us of their best technical judgment of a situation. It is interesting to note in this connection that once people have become convinced that we are actually living by this rule, we can get three time estimates much more rapidly and *accurately* than we could previously get one commitment.

The third rule for PERT operation is that there should be no changes in time estimates for the purpose of shortening a program. If a program must be shortened, time must be *bought*—with money, with risk, or by removing certain features. If it takes eight weeks to build a particular unit, management decision by itself won't change that fact. It is a fundamental principle that a time estimate for an activity should not be changed unless there is a significant change in the circumstances or requirements of that activity. It has been generally found that the original time estimates are more accurate than those resulting from second thoughts. To accept arbitrary time cuts from anyone would simply be a return to an ineffective planning procedure. The method for shortening programs should be realistic replanning. When a PERT plan shows that it is going to take 46 weeks to build a unit or meet an objective, this does not mean that it necessarily must take the 46 weeks. Rather, the plan indicates that it will take 46 weeks to build a unit in this particular way. There may be other ways involving more risk, or money, or more intelligence. The objective of PERT planning is to bring these three factors to bear effectively on the planning problem.

Lastly, PERT-planning consultant services should be provided by an administrative group established for the principal purpose of assisting and making more effective the individual's own efforts in planning his work in relation to the over-all program objectives. This group should be staffed by individuals whose experience and competence are commensurate with the people whom they are serving. There are two big advantages to this kind of arrangement. First, it contributes greatly to the effectiveness of communications with those implementing a particular program because the planning consultants are men with common experience who speak the same language and who are able to contribute actively and understand the work being done. Second, when a program is having difficulties which require action or decisions that are not being made or not being effectively pursued, the program planner is competent to recognize the situation. It has been found that the PERT technique voluntarily used and applied under these guidelines enables PERT planners to give better service to management by the simple procedure of giving better service to their men in the planning and control of their work.

# PERT/TIME AND THE MANAGER'S JOB •

KENNETH M. TEBO

M ANAGEMENT is always faced with the formidable task of making plans for programs, executing the plans, insuring that progress against the plans is satisfactory, and, finally, meeting all associated commitments. It is difficult, however, to look far enough ahead to see the total effect of current work slippages and other problems. Future results are largely determined by present program status and the intuitive judgment of the manager. In more complex programs, the human brain cannot compete with computers in digesting and sorting out the many operations into their proper interrelationships and dependencies. In such programs it is essential that (1) the plan be laid out as a total project by key personnel from the various functional organizations that contribute to the total effort; (2) the best judgments of the managers who are expert in the various segments of the plan be applied; (3) the interdependencies or coordinative efforts that are required to make the plan a success be considered and shown, where possible; and (4) a system is in being that ties all of these together to be processed by economical data-processing methods to give useful information for management decisions or actions.

Two important elements that have been omitted from these essentials are the resources (manpower, funds, facilities) needed to complete the program and the performance required to create the product. Although they are considered to be constant in the system to be discussed, some variations in either of these can be handled. In contrast to 30 years ago, managers still have the same responsibilities, but their jobs are more difficult since they are dealing with greater complexity and with tighter deadlines. Today's manager wants to know—and should demand to know—what his problems are in ample time to be able to do something

KENNETH M. TEBO is Director, Management Control and Analysis, AC Spark Plug Division, General Motors Corporation, Milwaukee, Wisconsin.

about them. He does not want to be faced with problems for which there is no solution except the application of time at the point when achievement is already at hand. Major General C. G. Medaris summed this up nicely when he stated:

> Give me a system that will wave yellow flags in my face when heading into trouble, but wave these early enough for me to do something about it. What I never want you to do is to wave a red flag at me, so that whole projects and programs must come to a screeching stop because of some unforeseen holdup.

The PERT technique is designed to prevent coming up to deadline dates without knowing that problems exist. In fact, it "waves the yellow flag" sufficiently in advance to let us do something about them.

### THE BASICS OF THE PERT SYSTEM

Let us look at PERT as it has evolved in practice. The basic theory of the PERT system is shown in Exhibit 1. In this simple diagram there are three paths leading to the key objective. The first path shows the assembly of a power supply unit and then the assembly of the power supply to the AJQ-4. The second path shows the assembly of a polar

### THE BASIS OF A PERT SYSTEM

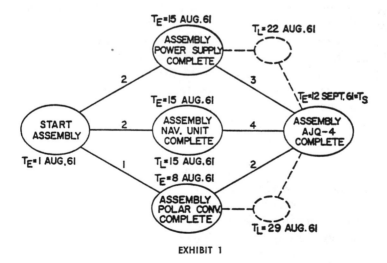

EXHIBIT 1

converter and then the assembly of that unit in AJQ-4. The third path
shows the assembly of a navigation unit and then the assembly of that
unit to AJQ-4. The times ($T_E$) shown on the activity lines are in normal
work weeks and are the expected times resulting from computer calculations on three time estimates. The equation used is:

$$T_E = \frac{a + 4m + b}{6}$$

in which *a* is the optimistic, *m* the most likely, and *b* the pessimistic time.

The longest path leading to the key objectives of assembling the complete AJQ-4 leads through the navigation unit. This is known as *the
critical path*—that is, the longest path through the network. A total of
six weeks is shown here. The other paths require less than six weeks
to accomplish. In practical terms this means that we could afford to
slip "Assembly power supply complete" by one week and "Assembly
polar converter complete" by three weeks and still reach the key objective on schedule.

If we suppose that the schedule is accelerated and we have to provide
the first AJQ-4 one week ahead of the schedule shown here, we know
immediately that we have to concentrate our management attention in
the critical path area in order to reduce time required. Since we have,
in effect, a slack of one week in one path and a slack of three weeks
in the other, this leads us to believe that if we could transfer manpower or resources from the three weeks' slack path to the critical path,
we might be able to meet the accelerated schedule. Management should
also consider overtime, double- or triple-shift operations, or other practical means to reduce times along the critical path in order to meet the
accelerated schedule, provided that these actions were not planned and
that the time estimates were not based thereon.

Let us see what the computer does for us in this operation. Anchor-
ing first on "time now," the computer "looks down" the network adding
up all the $T_E$'s and arranging them so that the expected completion date
of each event is calculated; hence, the time length of the longest path
and all other paths in the network are known. We see that the $T_E$ for
event "Assembly power supply complete" is August 15 and the $T_E$
for the key-objective event is September 12. Thus, by this forward-looking operation the expected time of completion of each event is obtained.

As a second operation, the computer anchors itself on the schedule
date of the key-objective event and looks back through the network in

order to determine the $T_L$ for each of the events in the network. ($T_L$ means the latest date by which this event must be completed in order not to affect the key-objective schedule.) Since the $T_L$ and $T_E$ for each event have been determined, the slack ($T_L - T_E$) for each of the events or activities is known. The computer then prints out $T_E$, $T_L$, and $T_L - T_E$ for each event in the network and arranges these in order of criticality with the most negative slack paths appearing first. Paths show-ing negative slack ($T_E$ is greater than $T_L$) means that time has got to be made up along these paths in the amount indicated in order to reach program-objective points on schedule.

Another operation that the computer does in PERT is to compute the probability of success for meeting scheduled dates. In Exhibit 2 we see where the addition of all the distribution curves for the activities in the network is a normal distribution curve with the nodal point giving

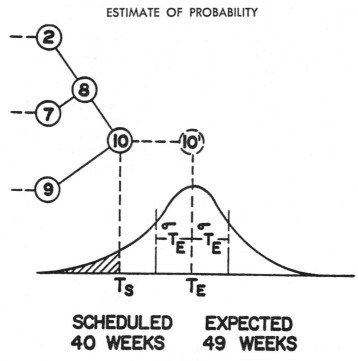

ESTIMATE OF PROBABILITY

SCHEDULED EXPECTED
40 WEEKS 49 WEEKS

EXHIBIT 2

the expected time of completion of the key-objective event. The schedule date ($T_S$) is ahead of the PERT $T_E$ date. The area under the distribution curve to the left of the $T_S$ line (the shaded area) is an estimate of the probability of success in meeting the objective schedule.

If PERT gave us nothing other than organized and directed planning, the system would be well worthwhile; however, we get much more in addition. We have found that the benefit derived from documenting the planning in PERT format has greatly increased the knowledge of the people working on a project. It forces comprehensive thinking and serves as an effective communications device.

### CONSTRUCTION OF A PERT NETWORK

The first step in developing a PERT network is to determine the key objective of the work. With the key-objective event established, it is then necessary to work backward determining those events that have to be completed in order to accomplish the task. All the major events back to "time now" are thus determined. For example, suppose the key objective is to ship the first prototype of a piece of complicated test equipment. Some of the events immediately prior to this would be the acceptance of the unit by the customer, the completion of factory tests, the certification of non-standard parts, the completion of packaging for shipment, and the completion of documentation. We would work back to what might be the first event in the network—the start of design. The events are then laid out on paper and connected by the activity lines in a dependency-sequence arrangement with all interrelationships shown.

For very complicated networks where the planning could become hazy and muddled, experience has shown that the backward approach is good up to a point—where the thinking becomes too tedious and frustrating to some. At this point a forward approach from "time now" should be undertaken. The two would then be dovetailed and a workable plan developed. The level of detail (number of events and activities) depends on the complexity of the equipment being developed and the level of management that would use the information generated. In our Milwaukee operations we have a merged network of about 4,000 events covering a bombing navigation system. This is being used for internal management control and integration of the over-all system for the Air Force. About 200 of the events are monitored for AC Spark Plug management review on a periodic basis.

A most important ingredient is having key planners and executives from the responsible functional areas on hand together with PERT specialists when the network is being developed and documented, for it is the users' plan and represents how they intend to fulfill commitments.

Upon completion of the network, the events are numbered, responsibilities (if desired) are assigned to the activities, interface activities with other tasks are shown, and three time estimates for each activity are obtained from those assigned or having the responsibility for each activity. The completed network is approved by the man in charge of the over-all project. The information is then converted to proper input form so that the data-processing operation can be completed, and outputs or printouts of the digested information can be obtained. In order to make it possible to follow progress visually and to determine wherein time can be saved (what activities are on negative slack paths), the computer printout information is manually transferred to the network.

A PERT SYSTEM IN OPERATION

How the PERT system is operating at AC Spark Plug is shown in Exhibit 3. The Management Control and Analysis Division assists the program offices in PERTing networks and obtaining time estimates. The network with its information is, however, the responsibility of the project office. Information to update the networks is given on a biweekly basis to the Management Control Division, which, in turn, puts it in the proper format for sending to the computer. After processing by the computer, a series of printouts is then made available to the Management Control and Analysis Division, to the program manager's office, and to those key managers who, the network indicates, are responsible for some phase of the project. All activities and events are arranged in relative order of criticality, with those having the most negative slack appearing first. Other printouts are made which show responsibility coding and those activities still to be completed.

The Management Control Division analyzes the computer outputs and reports independently to AC Spark Plug management. Copies of these analyses go to the program manager's office. This office is responsible for taking the action resulting from the PERT outputs and analyses

## PERT SYSTEM AT AC SPARK PLUG

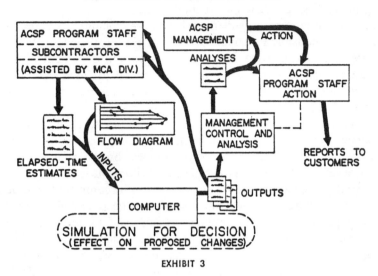

EXHIBIT 3

and for dealing with the customer. It is also in contact with subcontractors and associate contractors to insure that their portions of the program are being achieved in accordance with the plan. Raw data are furnished to the Management Division from the subcontractors and associate contractors who get direct copies of the computer outputs. The subcontractors are required to submit analyses of their programs. AC Spark Plug submits analyses of the over-all program to the customer. The main points brought out in these analyses are:

1. A discussion of the problems and their effect on the program.
2. The action that AC Spark Plug or the subcontractor is taking to solve the problem noted.
3. The action that is required of the customer or AC Spark Plug in order to keep the program on schedule.

### AN EVALUATION OF PERT

Experience has shown that PERT is most effective if (1) the technique is understood, (2) management supports it, (3) the inputs are objective and well prepared, (4) it is used for decision making, and (5) it is recognized as a tool and not a panacea. Advantages are that it:

1. Aids planning and shows progress.
2. Documents the plan.
3. Focuses the attention of management on problem areas ahead.
4. Increases communications.
5. Shows coordination required.
6. Saves time by the simple fact that thousands of events and activities can be processed through the computer in rapid fashion.
7. Integrates all elements of the program to the detail desired by the management concerned.
8. Possesses great flexibility.
9. Predicts probability of success.

The system is as good as the best judgment of the engineers, manufacturers, and others who make the networks and time estimates and provide the updating inputs to the computer. The computer is no substitute for the intelligence of man. If the information being processed is not the most objective possible, the computer doesn't know this and will produce outputs that are not the best that could be achieved.

For best results in developing the time estimates, schedules should be disregarded and, if possible, kept away from the room in which the time estimating is being done by those responsible for the activities. This will make it much easier to determine where the problems are in the project and where management should concentrate its attention. The only schedule dates that should appear on the network are those used for key-objective events so that the whole project can be evaluated to those dates. As an immediate benefit, it will be apparent where the use of overtime or a second shift or some additional resources should be considered—if these were not included in the original planning and time estimation.

The degree of management control desired can be reflected in the average length of time between events along main flows of effort or, if you will, by the most likely times required for the activities. In the Polaris program, these most likely times were kept at no more than six weeks nor less than two weeks wherever practicable. This means that an activity showing design effort which might, for example, take 15 weeks could be broken down to the design effort required for major components in parallel-path arrangements, or events could be inserted that could finitely determine percentage completion of design. There have been instances in other programs where some activities were about one day long. A very close management control was maintained in cases like these.

PERT is not a panacea for the ills of management. It is a very useful planning and evaluation tool, but it requires effort and attention in order to be valuable. The PERT system can be rigged or allowed to become inaccurate—but only for a short time, because failure to complete events and activities begins to show up. The time remaining to complete a job may be less as regards the calendar but about the same as regards PERT. Hence, any reasonable manager could determine that he has, for example, eight months' work to complete in six months. Sizable changes in time estimates become quite obvious and lead to re-evaluations. Objectivity is clearly essential in obtaining accurate information from the computer and is thus best for assisting in making proper management decisions.

A great deal of effort is being expended in various organizations to develop an extension of PERT which will include the estimated and actual costs of projects. One of the primary purposes of such a system would be to indicate the trade-offs between time and money, which would allow managers to recognize the impact of their decisions on both. One of the biggest problems to be resolved is the reconciliation of the cost estimating and accrual procedures and systems within companies to the PERT time concept of information gathering for complete projects. Several companies now relate manpower-loading information to the activities of the network. They thereby gain some concept of manpower needs, which is one of the major elements of total cost of a project.

Computerized line of balance systems are also being developed to give management a better analysis of production problems—especially to help anticipate what the production bottlenecks may be so that action can be initiated for solution in advance.

With these efforts to develop more encompassing systems, the PERT time system is continuing to expand. Many computer programs are in existence for processing PERT information. Others are also available for use on EAM equipment in small companies or for small projects. The growing acceptance of PERT is based on the effectiveness which it has shown in planning work, evaluating progress, and pinpointing potential problems well in advance of their occurrence. In short, it gives the manager a tool by which he can have the yellow flags instead of red ones waved in his face.

# THE PERT/COST TECHNIQUE •

GABRIEL N. STILIAN

$P$ERT/Cost is an extension of the PERT/Time technique. Its objective is to develop a plan of action for cost expenditures by applying the necessary cost-estimating techniques and to act as a monitor in determining variances—that is, where actual costs are different from planned costs.

The typical company budget is not a complete management control system for costs. Although the budget is an extremely important tool, it is primarily an accounting device which provides historical information for management review and evaluation. Hence, budget information does not meet the requirements of daily decision making: operating information that will be available at the time and in the manner required by supervisors and top managers to make decisions.

The management information which is provided by PERT/Cost, on the other hand, is designed precisely for this purpose. It helps managers find the trouble spots and critical areas that are now giving them cost problems or which may very likely do so in the future. In this way, the executive can give attention to a critical problem and thus prevent costs from overrunning, and he can anticipate potential problem areas in sufficient time to do something about them. He can also identify those activities from which he can divert resources in order to assist the more critical phases of the program. PERT/Cost is a means by which budgetary controls can be integrated directly with operational decisions.

With PERT/Cost we gather a body of information that is valuable for all levels of management and, at the same time, geared to the requirements of the particular responsibilities of each man involved in the program that is being controlled. By summarizing PERT/Cost information on a timely basis and presenting it in a decision-making form, the executive no longer has to review detailed data in order to evaluate program status. Rather, he has a report which is fitted to his situation, and he need go no further into detail unless he finds a problem which warrants additional analysis. In those cases where more information is needed, he is able to follow through the PERT/Cost reports to obtain the particular detail that he is seeking because of the interrelated nature of the PERT/Cost reporting system.

A PERT/COST SYSTEM

PERT/Cost is like any management planning and control method: it is a means by which a plan can be established and information can be generated which will help to control activities by showing where and by how much a plan is varying in actual operation from objectives. In other words, it establishes a basis for executive decision making and action. The PERT/Cost system adopted by the Defense Department and the National Aeronautics and Space Administration has a planning cycle which covers the following steps:

1. Establishing the project work-breakdown structure.
2. Defining tasks to be accomplished.
3. Preparing an account-code structure.
4. Constructing the PERT networks.
5. Estimating the activity times.
6. Scheduling the work.
7. Preparing resource and cost estimates.
8. Reviewing and revising the plan.

These elements of the planning cycle are considered to be the total requirement for the planning and control of time, costs, and resources in carrying out a management program.

The management control cycle is comprised of the following activities:

1. Approving the program plan, schedule, and budget.
2. Authorizing the work to be started.
3. Accumulating actual time and cost information.
4. Updating the plans as necessary.
5. Preparing PERT/Cost reports and information.
6. Analyzing the PERT reports and information.
7. Evaluating the status of the project.
8. Deciding on the necessary courses of action.
9. Revising the plans, schedules, and budgets as necessary.

## THE PROJECT WORK-BREAKDOWN STRUCTURE

The purposes of developing a work-breakdown structure are to find the project tasks that are to be performed and to establish their relationship to the program objectives. The project work breakdown acts, in a sense, as the design of a production line for the manufacture of a management program. In other words, just as a production plan is required for the manufacture of a physical product, so also a "production plan" is required for the most effective operation in the carrying out or "manufacturing" of a management program.

This situation has not been recognized by many executives in the past. However, the PERT/Cost system makes this very clear as it is carried out in practice. The PERT network and project work-breakdown structure develop a plan of action which shows precisely the activities and the method by which a program is to be accomplished. This is like a specially designed production line. When any variation from this methodology takes place, we find that we are deviating from the plan which has been deemed to be the most valuable.

Furthermore, the work breakdown establishes a basis for integrated cost and time planning and thereby provides a means for measurement and control of the work that is being structured. The most important aspect of the work-breakdown structure is that it provides the framework for gathering data concerning costs and schedule status for the different levels of management information that will be required. Thus, the work-breakdown structure is the first step in the development of the PERT network that will describe the program activities.

## PERT/COST REPORTS

The reports issuing from a PERT/Cost system must be interrelated and coordinated in order to provide a unified procedure for the presentation of decision information. Such a unified procedure allows for the analysis of information presented at the level of detail required and related specifically to the responsibility of the individual who will be using the information or the report for decision-making purposes. Consequently, PERT/Cost reports should present information for top-level management, middle management, and first-line management. Since the various reports are derived from the same basic data in all cases, no inaccurate or biased information is introduced. As a result, the manager who is using the information can feel certain that the data are tied into the rest of the reporting system that is being used for PERT planning and cost control purposes. Furthermore, the cost reports not only identify the problem areas in the program but also relate the individual who is responsible for the problem. The reports lead naturally and easily to executive decision and action as required.

It is important for each company to set up its own information requirements. Nevertheless, some profit can be derived from a discussion of the PERT/Cost reports developed in the PERT/Cost system of the Defense Department and NASA because they are indicative of the kinds that can be used effectively. The emphasis can be varied depending upon the particular needs of the company, as can the format and the approach in terms of developing the information. Nevertheless, the basic documents are, in one way or another, relevant to the objectives of the PERT/Cost management information system.

There are five kinds of reports that are particularly important:
1. A management summary report, which is aimed at a particular management level or executive responsibility.
2. A manpower report, which consists of the manpower-loading report and the manpower-loading display.
3. Milestone reporting, which shows an over-all picture of the current year's activities in terms of the accomplishment of major events and in terms of what the program as a whole looks like up to the point of completion.
4. Predictive reports, which develop trends and are tied into time in one case and cost in the other. There is a schedule outlook report which shows the trend of the projected schedule for the completion of the total project as it is seen on each monthly report date. The cost outlook report does the same thing for costs, showing the trend. of the projected cost overrun or underrun for the completion of the total project as seen at the time of reporting.
5. A cost-of-work report, which is a presentation of actual expenditures and commitments to date against budgeted rate of expenditures, usually presented in a graphic manner. This report also shows the estimates for the work performed to date.

It would be incorrect to assume that these reports are the total information output in PERT/Cost or the only way to structure a PERT/Cost system. Rather, they are one approach to a reporting structure that can help provide the timely information that is required for accurate and precise decision making. The important part of this reporting system is that each of the individual reports is integrated and interrelated with the others so that they meet a specific need in terms of guiding the manager in his program decisions and activities.

*Management summary report.* The PERT/Cost management summary report does not produce all the information required at the particular management level that is being covered. Information is generated in other ways than reports. In many instances, action is taken in a program even before a report which indicates the necessity for this type of action is developed. Information is transmitted on a more timely basis by word of mouth and by discussions in program planning and control meetings which are tied in with the PERT/Cost reporting system. Also, the reports are often accompanied by written analysis and recommendations for action.

The summary report (see Exhibit 1) has as its objective the presentation of an over-all time and cost schedule for both the program as a whole and each of the major elements of the program. It highlights the areas where problems seem to be arising and which will therefore require management attention. It singles out problems of time-schedule slippage and cost overruns. Furthermore, the amount of actual slippage or cost variance is indicated to show the difference between the established schedule for the completion of the project and the present expected date for project completion. It indicates the actual cost overrun or underrun to date by a comparison of the estimated cost with actual costs for the work performed. This leads to the anticipated cost variance for the total project, which can be obtained by analyzing the original cost estimate for the project in relation to the actual costs plus the costs estimated to complete the total program.

When each responsible executive is presented with this kind of summary report relating to his particular responsibility, he is in a stronger position to make the correct decisions at the correct time and thereby operate his part of the program at its most profitable level. Since this can be done for the first-line manager as well as middle and top management, we find that we have a complete and comprehensive system for the integration of management information for decision making, and the management summary report is a key factor in accomplishing this.

## MANAGEMENT SUMMARY REPORT

| | PROGRAM: | | SUMMARY LEVEL: | | REPORT COVERS THE PERIOD: |
|---|---|---|---|---|---|
| | PROJECT: | | CONTRACTOR: | CONTRACT NUMBER | DATE THIS REPORT: |

Schedule legend:

Δ = Scheduled completion date of total item
E = Earliest completion date  } of most critical
L = Latest completion date  } element within item

1961 J A S O N D | 1962 J F M A M J J A S O N D | 1963 J F M A M J

| ITEM | COST OF WORK | | | | | | SCHEDULE | DAY | SLACK STATUS (Weeks) | REMARKS |
|---|---|---|---|---|---|---|---|---|---|---|
| | WORK PERFORMED TO DATE $ | | | TOTALS AT COMPLETION $ | | | | | | |
| | Original Estimate | Actual Costs | Overrun (Underrun) | Contract Estimate | Latest Revised Estimate | Projected Overrun (Underrun) | | | | |

REMARKS:
S = Schedule Slippage
O = Cost Overrun
U = Cost Underrun

EXHIBIT 1

*Manpower-loading reports and displays.* The PERT/Cost system is often operated without the manpower-loading information that is related directly to the events that are being accomplished in the PERT network. However, when these reports and displays are not used, there is the danger that the complete picture will not be available to the manager and that he will not have the precision that is essential in allocating manpower. Furthermore, they help in the shifting of resources within particular skills from one activity to another in order to gain the maximum value for the program at least cost.

The manpower reports (see Exhibit 2) show the plan for assignments and are usually developed for each job description or skill requirement. They are used by executives to plan the allocation of personnel and to establish the need for additional employees, overtime, rescheduling, or whatever else is essential to make the program operate at the desired level of performance. The manpower-loading display (Exhibit 3) shows the total requirements for manpower, while the manpower-loading report shows the allocation of man-hours to the various work packages or groups of activities as shown by the charge number, which is the accounting code for the work packages. This report provides the manager with the means by which he can smooth and balance idle manpower, shift it to situations that are more critical, and thereby utilize skills and available man-hours to better advantage.

The manpower-loading display makes it possible to minimize over-

### MANPOWER-LOADING REPORT

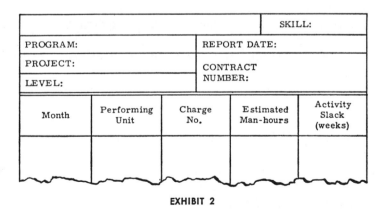

| | | | SKILL: | |
|---|---|---|---|---|
| PROGRAM: | | REPORT DATE: | | |
| PROJECT: | | CONTRACT NUMBER: | | |
| LEVEL: | | | | |
| Month | Performing Unit | Charge No. | Estimated Man-hours | Activity Slack (weeks) |
| | | | | |

EXHIBIT 2

## MANPOWER-LOADING DISPLAY

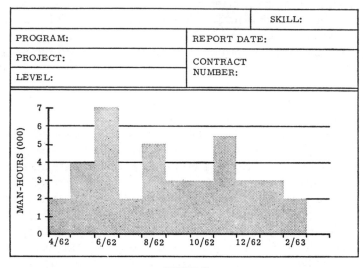

EXHIBIT 3

time by allocating resources from one month to another or by rescheduling slack activities so that they are moved to another period of time. This will allow activities to be accomplished with available manpower and, since the activities are not on the critical path, prevent delaying the over-all program.

*Cost-of-work reports.* The cost-of-work report (Exhibit 4) develops the information necessary for the following:

1. Budgeted costs: the amount of money required to accomplish the program.
2. Committed costs: the actual costs that are committed or expended to date.
3. Cost performance and progress: the estimate for the work performed and the progress to date based on original estimates.
4. Projected costs to complete: the estimated cost to complete the program based on actual costs to date and estimated costs for the balance of the program.

The cost-of-work report provides a means of analyzing the original estimate that was prepared for the program to see whether the actual costs to date are in line with the estimated costs. The cost-of-work report

## COST-OF-WORK REPORT

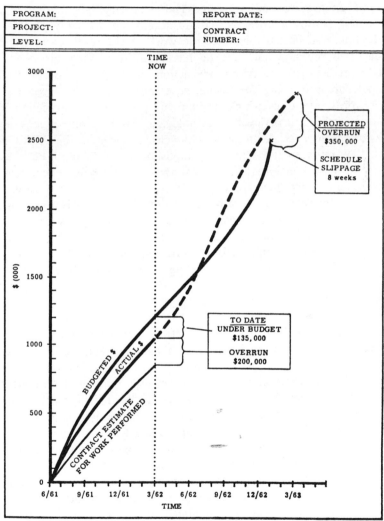

| PROGRAM: | REPORT DATE: |
|---|---|
| PROJECT: | CONTRACT |
| LEVEL: | NUMBER: |

Budgeted \$ = Planned rate of expenditure
Actual \$   = Expenditures & commitments made to date

**EXHIBIT 4**

presents its information graphically and in a simple summary fashion.

*Outlook reports for schedule and costs.* These reports (Exhibits 5 and 6) are a graphic means of predicting a cost overrun or a time slippage on the over-all program. The necessary information is accumulated to show the trends that are developing. Monthly projections of the time and cost to complete the work of the program enable the manager to see how effective he has been in making his decisions and to predict whether or not the actions he is taking to control his schedule are producing the results he wants. The outlook reports, in other words, are tools which develop his precision in projecting into future as well as in reviewing and analyzing his previous effectiveness.

*Milestone reports.* A milestone is a selected event in the PERT network that represents a major accomplishment. It is used both as a target and as a benchmark in evaluating results. It helps executives to know exactly how they are doing. In some instances it is desirable to include this type of information in the PERT/Cost management summary report, but in others separate milestone reports can be developed. These milestone reports are generally submitted with a written analysis: action accomplished on schedule and action planned are explained. Because they give a feeling for the over-all project, they help to fit the smaller components into the total picture, which sometimes can be very valuable to the operating executive.

However, these reports are of little value unless they show by some means what action is required, when it is required, and on what activities or milestones it is required. Even though each milestone scheduled during the life of a program or during the period of a year may be marked off, this information in itself serves little purpose. Consequently, it can be seen that the reporting system for the PERT/Cost management information and control system must be flexible. The objective is to provide information for decision making to the executive responsible for a particular phase of the total program: information that allows him to see far enough into the future to take preventive and corrective action to insure that slippages of time and cost overruns do not occur. This is not budget information; it is information that is simple, timely, and precise—and aimed at the specific decision that the executive must deal with. It can then be integrated with his experience and his creative thinking to produce the most profitable management action and decision making that can be expected of him.

## COST OUTLOOK REPORT

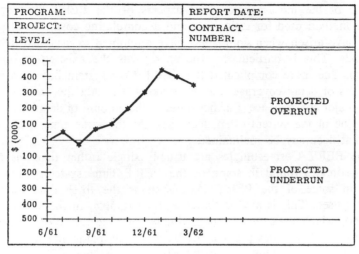

EXHIBIT 5

## SCHEDULE OUTLOOK REPORT

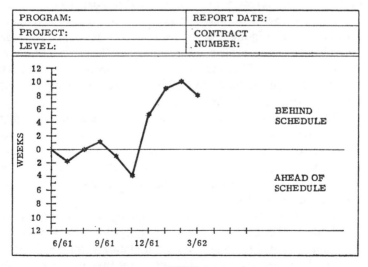

EXHIBIT 6

METHODS FOR ESTIMATING AND ACCUMULATING COST INFORMATION

One of the most controversial aspects of the PERT/Cost system is the method used for estimating and accumulating costs; many problems have arisen when companies have attempted to establish detailed methods. This is particularly true as regards the existing accounting system. The more complicated the PERT/Cost system has been made in terms of detail coverage, the more likely it is that the problems will be of major consequence. Furthermore, as the amount of detail increases, the value of the system often decreases. At the same time it is essential that accuracy be maintained.

The PERT/Cost estimates are usually single rather than the three time estimates found in some of the PERT/Time systems. However, even in some of the PERT/Time systems the three time estimates are not used. This is always the case, for example, in the critical path method, which uses only single estimates of time and cost. Nevertheless, the cost estimates provide the basis for the plans and the controls concerning costs. They are ordinarily made in the PERT planning sessions.

Estimates of manpower, materials, and other resources required to accomplish a group of activities are developed on the PERT network. The estimates of resources are then converted to costs so as to establish the direct cost of each work package (which is a group of activities or a major activity). The indirect costs are added to the work packages or to the total cost of the project—depending on the accounting method used by the company. Thus the work packages serve as benchmarks so that the cost status of the program can be evaluated by comparing actual costs with the original estimates.

A PERT/Cost estimating form (Exhibit 7) is used in collecting the information for cost and resource estimating. It can also be used to collect all the direct cost data for each work package and as a basis for computer input or for manual calculations. The dollar estimates are prepared from the requirements for manpower, materials, equipment, services, and other resouces.

In addition, it is necessary to make estimates on a monthly or other periodic basis to develop cost data to complete each work package that has been started. Cost and resource updating work sheets are used in preparing these cost estimates. This constant updating is necessary in

## PERT/COST ESTIMATING FORM

| RESPONSIBLE UNIT: | DATE: | CHARGE NO. |
|---|---|---|
| DESCRIPTION: | | SUMMARY NO. |

| EVENT NO. | PERT TIME ESTIMATES | SCHEDULED ELAPSED TIME | SCHEDULE |
|---|---|---|---|
| Beginning: (first) Ending: (last) | Optimistic: Most Likely: Pessimistic: | | Start Date: End Date: |

### ESTIMATED MANPOWER (HRS.) AND DIRECT COSTS ($)

| IDENTIFICATION | | | MONTHS beginning with start date | | | | | | | | | | | |
|---|---|---|---|---|---|---|---|---|---|---|---|---|---|---|
| cc Hours or $ Code | cc-cc Performing Unit | cc-cc Resource Code | cc-cc 1 | cc-cc 2 | cc-cc 3 | cc-cc 4 | cc-cc 5 | cc-cc 6 | cc-cc 7 | cc-cc 8 | cc-cc 9 | cc-cc 10 | cc-cc 11 | cc-cc 12 |
| | | | | | | | | | | | | | | |
| | | | | | | | | | | | | | | |
| | | | | | | | | | | | | | | |
| | | | | | | | | | | | | | | |
| | | | | | | | | | | | | | | |
| | | | | | | | | | | | | | | |
| | | | | | | | | | | | | | | |
| | | | | | | | | | | | | | | |
| | | | | | | | | | | | | | | |

START DATE occurs during this month.

"H"=Man-hours
"D"=Direct Dollars
"T"=Total Dollars

ESTIMATOR _____

APPROVED _____

DATE _____

**EXHIBIT 7**

order to keep the system working. The time schedule of each activity in a work package is examined, and all the schedule slippages are analyzed to establish whether original time and cost estimates need to be revamped. If the activity is on schedule and can be completed within the cost originally planned for the work package, that will be readily apparent. However, schedule slippages that delay the performance of work call for revised cost estimates and a reallocation of resources.

In some cases, cost estimating is done simultaneously with time estimating. In others, the scheduling is completed before cost estimates are developed. In any case, the updating process is necessary if activities are changed or added, if work is completed behind or ahead of schedule, or if time and cost estimates for unfinished work need to be revised.

The updating is facilitated by establishing specific review dates. Moreover, by assigning responsibility to individuals who are involved in the program, estimates can more easily be prepared and revised, and they are more likely to be kept up to date quickly and accurately. The cost and resource updating work sheet can be used as a detailed record of current costs and resource estimates and as a guide for the preparation of the latest revised estimates. The report is prepared periodically for each responsible department performing work on the program. It includes a listing of the latest estimates from the PERT/Cost estimating forms of the previous month. Hence each new work sheet shows estimates for future months only.

A budget authorization form is used in assigning budgets to accounts. Thereafter it is used for transferring budgets between accounts. It also helps in adding or subtracting current estimates for an account and is a means of relating the PERT/Cost system to the budget. In this way the total planning and control system is properly integrated and kept up to date as is necessary for effective decision making and budget control.

# SECTION III: PRACTICAL EXPERIENCE WITH PERT

*The obvious second step for the line manager who is considering the use of PERT is to determine what success other business men have achieved with it. In this section, managers who have had actual experience with PERT present case studies in the application of this technique to business situations. They also share some of the lessons they have learned and reveal a number of suggestions for improving PERT even further.*

# A DYNAMIC PROJECT
# CONTROL METHOD •

## LEONARD P. HARTUNG

---

SOME TIME AGO the IBM Federal Systems Division Space Guidance Center realized the need for a planning technique that would guide the individual contributor and management in realistically planning the work to be performed and measure performance against these plans. What we wanted was a management tool that would (1) aid planning; (2) improve communications; (3) focus attention on coordination actions; (4) display status and progress; (5) highlight areas for management attention; (6) forecast probability of success; (7) save time in the accomplishment of contract tasks; and (8) allow evaluation of responsible departments and contracts. In addition, we needed the following:

1. A systematic method of planning R&D progress in terms of time, manpower and money.
2. A way of producing in a very short time many plans that would depict the input of changes in manpower, materials, facilities, and so forth and the establishment of the work responsibilities which are required to control any R&D program.
3. A means of supplying information so that we would have a plan for looking ahead in order to take immediate corrective action on all problems as they become known.
4. A systematic way of keeping all levels of management informed of the work plan.
5. A program that would require a minimum of training.
6. A single reporting system that would allow objective evaluation and insure positive communication.

---

LEONARD P. HARTUNG is Manager, Program Analysis and Review Department, International Business Machines Corporation, Owego, New York.

In the past, we had attempted to obtain the desired degree of management control in large and complex R&D programs by using the Gantt and milestone reporting techniques. With the Gantt charts, we defined program objectives by using bars but found it very difficult to confirm progress against a bar representing a broad effort over a long period of time. To obtain better control, we next added milestones at various points on the bars, but we were still unable to indicte the interrelationship of tasks.

In order to give us complete management control of our programs, top management decided to take advantage of the techniques found in PERT, which has been called the most effective management tool yet conceived for planning and evaluating progress in the development of complex R&D systems. It is a technique that defines and integrates what must be done to accomplish program objectives on time and that makes use of computers to assimilate and simulate massive amounts of data to obtain the best plan. It is also a technique that lends itself readily to the calculation of all data by hand.

We now have in PERT a tool by which the individual becomes a part of the management team and in which he has the responsibility for managing his assigned task. The basic objectives of the PERT technique are: (1) orderliness and consistency in planning and evaluating all areas of a program; (2) early identification of all potential trouble areas arising within the project; and (3) early positive identification for the initiation of corrective action to be taken by the organization having operational responsibility. PERT is also a quantitative tool that identifies problem areas, utilizes time to best advantage, is readily adaptable to R&D programs, is favored by technical people, and keeps current with program-planning changes.

The basic requirement of the PERT technique is of course the network, which consists of time estimates and a diagrammatic representation of the program. The network shows the sequence and interrelationship of significant events in achieving end objectives under plant-resource applications and performance specifications. Time is associated with the pertinent events that must occur during a program. Resources pertain to interrelated plans such as manpower plans, facilities plans, budget cost-requirement plans, and financial plans relating to sources of funds; performance specifications pertain to the technical performance of the system, subsystems, and components.

## A MANAGEMENT PHILOSOPHY FOR WEAPONS SYSTEMS

At IBM we manage our weapon-systems programs by following a management philosophy that involves the functions of designing, developing, testing, producing, training, supporting, and maintaining. In order to implement our philosophy, we use the five elements of management: planning, organizing, directing, coordinating, and controlling. These elements are used as a means of organizing and employing resources to accomplish predetermined objectives by use of the PERT technique.

1. *Planning.* In industry, management is measured in terms of end items produced or profits resulting from end items produced, and end objectives cannot be reached unless a mangement plan is in effect. Therefore, it is axiomatic to say that management efforts start with planning, which is the hard-thinking process of selecting the best line of action to accomplish the assigned mission. Since planning is the key to progress, to what extent must we plan for PERT? To be effective, PERT planning is required on all levels of management and must include: executive management, project office, divisions (engineering, manufacturing, quality and reliability), support areas (training, documentation, procurement, components), plant resources, departments, and individuals. Planning, then, consists of the following seven steps:
   a. Objective: determine what the objective is; what is supposed to be accomplished.
   b. Analysis: get the facts; define what is required to reach the objectives.
   c. Evaluation: study various ways to reach the end objective; select the best plan.
   d. Improvement: determine better ways to reach the end objective.
   e. Testing: study the plan through simulation.
   f. Trial: check for weak areas; make sure that everyone knows and uses the plan.
   g. Application: start the project; follow up to see that the plan is being adhered to.
2. *Organizing.* After selecting a line of action by means of the PERT

technique, operating department managers bring together the elements which will enable them to work out that line of action. They properly organize and program the elements. In other words, they interrelate the factors and elements pertinent to the line of action in a systematic and practical way.

3. *Directing.* To carry out objectives effectively, each operating department manager must see to it that positive directions are given to assigned personnel having task responsibilities so that they will know what to do.

4. *Coordinating.* It is the responsibility of the project office to coordinate the weapon systems program tasks by effectively working with managers having task responsibilities. In turn, the operating department managers coordinate their assigned tasks.

5. *Controlling.* The last element of mangement is that of controlling, which makes it imperative that procedures be established to insure that progress is made in accordance with the plan depicted by the PERT network.

## PERT ORGANIZATION

The functional departments charged with the implementation and the continuance of the PERT techniques at IBM are classified into two general groups. The Service group provides the necessary program-phasing plans, instructions, training, computer services, technical advice, and general services to the operating group to effect and maintain the PERT technique. The Operating group conducts the actual work to effect applicable program objectives, as listed in the statement of work, through use of the PERT technique. It performs its tasks in accordance with the plan as depicted by PERT networks and analysis reports.

IBM uses the "project office" concept which establishes a single responsible authority to manage weapon-systems programs. The accompanying exhibit is an organization chart depicting the role of the planning steering group and its relationship to the project office and the operating department coordinators. Program planning, then, is a joint effort between the service and operating groups. Briefly, the responsibilities of each major group are as follows:

1. The project office has the prime responsibility of producing all

## PERT ORGANIZATION

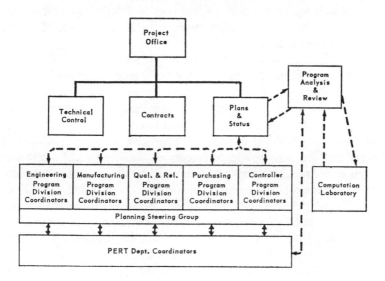

program plans, statements of work, and so forth. It also coordinates its own activities and those of all other affected departments to assure that the resultant program satisfies the contractor's requirements and efficient plant operation. It thereby exercises over-all management cognizance of all projects being pursued at IBM Owego.

2. .The Program Analysis and Review Department (PAR) consists primarily of program evaluation review analysts who are specialists selected from each functional division. They are assigned specific programs and are available for consultation regarding items pertaining to their specialty. Within its intended field, PAR is in a position to survey and make recommendations for improving the work plan depicted by the PERT technique. The PAR analyst also assists the project office in collecting and formalizing task statements and in performing program analysis.

3. The project office planning coordinator (plans and status) has as his basic responsibilities the following:

   *a.* To establish program requirements after collaborating with the appropriate project office manager and other top management personnel concerned.

    *b.* To formulate project concepts and philosophy, establish project policies, and assign project responsibilities with the assistance of the project office planning steering group, of which he is the chairman.

    *c.* To effect the work program by providing a planning document for its accomplishment, with the assistance of the project office planning steering group.

    *d.* To assume responsibility for managing and approving all project office efforts directly concerned with program planning.

4. The planning steering group (program division coordinators) is comprised of responsible management and technical personnel from each functional area and is chaired by the project office planning coordinator. This group coordinates the working procedures and planning activities of the various departments in accordance with the PERT technique. Area coordinators are assigned to members of the planning steering group by the manager of the functional department. The members of the steering group have a threefold responsibility in assisting the project office planning coordinator in the formulation of over-all policies pertaining to the program; implementing and maintaining those policies in their area of responsibility; and reviewing objectives and performance and preparing evaluation reports for top management decision making. This group also outlines the job to be done and provides detailed system and subsystem parameters which include the job description, performance requirements, task measurement, and the technical approach.

5. The operating department managers have as their basic responsibility to plan the work programs related to each project, as outlined by the applicable functional member of the steering group, by utilizing the PERT technique.

6. The operating department coordinators are assigned, by each manager in his area, the responsibility for implementing and maintaining the PERT technique. The coordinators work closely with department personnel who have the responsibility for completing the assigned tasks. They also maintain close liaison with the applicable functional member of the project office planning steering group or area coordinator to effect program objectives by use of the PERT technique.

## NETWORK DEVELOPMENT

In implementing and maintaining the PERT technique, IBM follows a definite procedure. At the inception of a program, the project office planning steering group delineates parameters for development planning. These parameters are used by operating departments to develop PERT networks based on the statement of work, which provides the framework against which IBM reports schedule position and future programing status to the customer.

For the PERT technique to be effective, a well-designed plan of control for each major functional activity must be formulated. It consists of four elements: the objective, establishing and clearly defining what is to be accomplished; a procedure, specifying how, when, and by whom the objective is to be attained; the criteria, determining what constitutes good performance or a preconceived opinion of how well the job should be done; and an appraisal, evaluating how well the job was done on the basis of results which are obtained from PERT output analysis sheets.

Before a weapon-systems program can be PERTed, a PERT development plan is effected by the project office planning steering group. It obtains the support of top management and the project office for the program to be PERTed; conducts a survey of the organizational approaches; makes another survey, with the personnel having program responsibility, in order to prepare a PERT operating manual and training manual and to establish a training program; adapts the program to cover all operating departments; and obtains network data to implement PERT for program accomplishment. When these requirements are fulfilled, we are then ready to start network planning.

The foundation of the PERT technique is the network. To be effective, networks are developed on the basis of the statement of work established by the project office. PERT network planning should be done without the constraint of a schedule and on the level where the work is to be performed. If a schedule is used, PERT then becomes a mere reporting tool. Therefore, by the use of PERT we establish a network schedule which depicts the complete statement of work in a single network plan.

STEP 1: THE PLAN STRUCTURE

The first step in network development is to prepare a plan structure, based on the program statement of work which outlines the total job to be accomplished by IBM. Then a summary network is prepared. Some exponents of PERT state that we should develop a summary network for the total weapon-systems program first and then progress to a detailed network. Others believe that it is best to start at the detailed level and work up to the program level. At IBM, at the start of a program, we make a rough summary network to depict the interrelationship of major milestones in the creation of the weapon system, but the final integrated summary network is made from the completed detailed networks. This integrated network shows the relationship of each detailed network to the others.

The plan structure and summary network are then forwarded to operating departments, where the operating department coordinator and the members of the operating department project team prepare the detailed plan structure and networks which must represent the plan for doing the work. To obtain a positive degree of control, it is important that members of project teams be accountable for (1) preparing the network for the assigned task; (2) defining event and activity descriptions; (3) estimating the three time estimates; (4) providing current input data; and (5) providing analysis and corrective action from network output data.

This means that members of project teams must have a hand in the planning if they are to accept a task responsibility. The system becomes more effective when information is provided to these members for use in task evaluation, for noting progress, and for replanning to improve the network event schedule.

STEP 2: PLANNING THE EVENT CHECKLIST

The second step is to make a listing of all input, action, and output events for the assigned task. Every type of specification, drawing, report, and so on is listed, with a column spacing to designate whether the event is an input, action, or output. An action event is one that is to be accomplished by the action department. Input and output events of an action department are called interfacing events, since they are common to more than one department network and they are necessary to accomplish the end objective. The inputs required by an action department are the outputs of another action department and vice versa. Therefore, it is important that action departments coordinate their efforts to insure compatibility of events for complete and positive interfacing. Output events are always numbered by the action department.

STEP 3: PROGRAM PLANNING SHEET

The information from the checklist is time-sequenced on program-planning sheets to the desired plan-structure level.

STEP 4: PERT NETWORK

*Network planning.* After the initial planning is completed, the information is transposed from program planning sheets to a PERT network-planning sheet in the form of input, action, and output events. These are placed along the horizontal axis roughly according to schedule relationships depicted on the planning sheets. At IBM, the levels of networks used depend upon the particular program, which, in most cases, covers a range of at least three levels (system, subsystem, equipment, set, unit, assembly, subassembly, or part).

When the functional approach is used, separate networks are prepared by each functional department, such as systems engineering, systems integration, test equipment engineering, manufacturing, or quality control and reliability—or for each major piece of hardware. Thus we can effect changes on individual networks and also make a rapid analysis and evaluation of each network on an independent basis. When the team approach is employed, a group of the best technical people from each functional department participate. This results in a more positive planning approach and reduces the chances of misunderstanding what constitutes an effective network.

On a new proposal or a new R&D program, the network is created by working from the end objective to time now; while on an R&D program that has already been started, it is best to work from time now to the end objective. We have found that it takes about 96 man-hours to complete a 400-event network. We insure that networks are prepared down to the level of first-line supervision. Areas having the greatest program-delay potential are charted in much more detail than those areas which play a lesser role.

*Events.* The flow plan consists of events that can be established as points in time when a decision is made. No work is accomplished at these points, since they are considered milestones or objectives. Clearly defined, they include such items as the issuance of task outlines, the approval of final drawings, the completion of design; or the completion of procurement. A satisfactory event must be (1) positive, specific, tangible, and meaningful to the project; (2) definitely distinguishable at a specific point in time; and (3) readily understood by all concerned with the project.

*Activities.* Activities represent work, while events represent specific accomplishments that are the result of work. The events on the PERT network are connected by activity lines represented by arrows to show the flow and interrelationship between time now and an event. An activity, then, is a time-consuming element in the development process. The flow plan is formulated so that all activities lead to an objective event. Activities start and end with a decision. By definition, an activity has a preceding event, which is the starting point, and a succeeding event, which is the end point. The elapsed time for each activity indicates the interval during which actual work is accomplished. It is most important that activities be precisely defined in order to obtain accurate time estimates. A satisfactory activity must (1) be a positive, specific, tangible, and meaningful effort; (2) be such that the primary responsibility for the effort can be determined; (3) have a description understandable by all; and (4) have a time span in accordance with PAR instructions.

*Time estimates.* To complete the network, we must estimate the elapsed time necessary to complete an activity in a specified manner. In obtaining raw data from the engineers, we felt that more realistic evaluations could be made if three estimates for each activity were obtained. This practice was designated to help disassociate the engineer from his built-in knowledge of the existing schedules and to provide more information concerning the inherent difficulties and variability in the activity being estimated. Consequently, three numbers designated as optimistic, pessimistic, and most likely are obtained for each activity. These times are called activity times.

1. The optimistic time estimate is designated by the letter "a" and is the best time to complete the activity. If the activity were

repeated 100 times, this would be the best time of the 100-time operation with a probability of 1/100.

2. The pessimistic estimate is designated by the letter "b" and is the longest time that the activity will take, or it is the worst time in the 100-time operation with a probability of 1/100.

3. The most likely estimate is designated by the letter "m" and is the most likely estimate if only one were to be given. It is the time that would occur most often if the activity were repeated 100 times under the same conditions.

At IBM the three time estimates are obtained in the following order: optimistic, pessimistic, and most likely. However, whenever they are written, the order is optimistic, most likely, and pessimistic. The PERT mean time ($t_e$) to complete an activity is calculated by use of the following formula:

$$t_e = \frac{a + 4m + b}{6}$$

The $t_e$ from the time-distribution beta curve has about a 50-50 chance of being met. Therefore, the completed network depicts the plan that is to be used to complete the project with the addition of time, and it depicts a critical path (the longest path in the network) that limits the end objective or completion date and diverts the slack paths.

To obtain satisfactory time estimates, a number of requirements must be fulfilled. Estimates should:

1. Be reported in weeks and tenths of weeks, being based on elapsed-time estimates.

2. Be based on presently available manpower and resources.

3. Be made on the premise that the activity lies on the critical path.

4. Relate to all resource applications: number, skill, and talent of personnel required: facilities; equipment; materials; and so forth.

5. Be made only by the individual who is assigned the work responsibility or by an individual who is capable of doing that work.

6. Be entered above each activity line to which they apply.

*Event numbering.* After completion of time estimates, network events are numbered randomly or reviewed sequentially for accuracy and reasonableness by the department planning coordinator. At IBM, we use the random-numbering system because of its ease of application. For a network to be effective, the sequence of events should be checked for logical planning.

STEP 5: PREPARATION OF INFORMATION WORK SHEET

The data from the completed network is then transposed to a PERT information work sheet, which is used to provide both original and updating information to the computation center. All entries on the input data sheets are closely checked to insure accuracy of data transposed from the applicable network. Department network charts are maintained by appropriate personnel in order to provide reference and back-up material for the data submitted through the input data sheet. Detail networks are integrated as required by management or customers.

At IBM we use a time-now biweekly reporting system. Time now relates to activities in progress which are defined as having completed predecessor events and incompleted successor events. These activities are evaluated in terms of the amount of work remaining to be accomplished in order to complete the task. New time estimates are used to reflect the three times required from the report cut-off date to the completion of the activity under evaluation.

STEP 6: COMPUTER OUTPUTS

The heart of the PERT system is the computer, which facilitates and maintains the position of current program progress with an emphasis upon critical paths. We use the IBM 7090 computer in our PERT operation. After the computer processes the PERT data, management is provided with a timely, accurate series of reports that not only pinpoint present progress but also forecast the future of the program being analyzed. It has been found that the rewards of PERT are in direct proportion to the use and importance management attaches to these computer outputs. Since the PERT networks represent the plan for accomplishing the over-all task, the PERT technique will be more effective if the computer output sheets are also used for activity scheduling. The computer role is as follows:

    A. Inputs:
        1. Periodic time estimates or re-estimates (optimistic, most likely, and pessimistic).
        2. Activity changes:
            *a.* Additions.
            *b.* Deletions.
            *c.* Completions.

    *d.* Re-estimates, which should not be made unless there is
a change in work contract or the rate of application of
resources. Re-estimating should be done under only the
following conditions:
    (1) Plans are revised.
    (2) New resources (additional manpower or a second-
or third-shift operation) are introduced.
    (3) Personnel are added or reduced.
    (4) Technical difficulties arise.
    (5) Technical breakthroughs are experienced.
    (6) Overtime is authorized.

B. Outputs:
1. Expected completion date for each event ($T_E$).
2. Latest allowable date for each event ($T_L$).
3. Slack and critical areas ($T_L - T_E$) expressed in weeks.
4. Probability ($P_R$) of meeting schedule date ($T_S$).

For PERT to be effective the computer printouts should be distributed
not earlier than 24 hours after the input information is received by the
PAR department nor later than 48 hours. Typical computer printouts
(each of which lends itself to independent analysis and yet forms an
integral portion of the complete program picture) are in the following
forms:

1. Activity listing by predecessor-successor event number. This printout represents the complete network of events. All the predecessor
events are printed in succeeding order by event number.
2. Ending event by successor event number and predecessor event
number. This is sometimes referred to as a tab run and provides
easy access to any activity or event through the successor event
number which is printed out in numerical sequence.
3. Ending event by paths of criticality. This is a printout of slack
criticality, listing negative slack paths in descending order and
positive slack paths in ascending order.
4. Ending event by schedule or latest allowable date and successor
event number. This is a printout of the actual completion date
($T_C$) of successor events by date sequence compared to allowed
date ($T_L$) for the same event. When time now (date of report)
is reached and completion date is not available, the order then
changes and is in date sequence by allowed date. Thus, with the

time-now date as a reference, it is easy to determine which events should have been completed and were not.

5. Ending event by department, schedule, or latest allowable date and successor event. This is a printout of the actual completion date and the allowable date by date sequence for each department.

6. Projected departmental manpower summary. This is a printout of department manpower requirements for each activity by department and number sequence of predecessor event.

7. Summary printout run by successor event number and predecessor event number. This is a printout of the major events from detail networks which permits top management to grasp quickly the essential status of the total program in summary form. The summary presentation is also a means by which simulated data may be used for management decision making.

*Critical paths.* The critical path of a network is the longest path in the network from the base line or time now to the end objective. It represents the sequence of activities and events which require the greatest amount of time for accomplishment. It is possible to have more than one critical path. Where several paths exist, as many as possible should be analyzed to evaluate the resulting action of changing one or more events along the paths as a means of improving the schedule.

Criticality is measured in times of negative, zero, or positive slack. Positive slack indicates an ahead-of-schedule condition or the amount of time an event can be delayed without adversely affecting the schedule of the end objective. Negative slack indicates a behind-schedule condition; while zero slack indicates an on-schedule condition with a probability of 0.5. Negative slack occurs when the total activity mean time along the critical path is greater than the time available to meet program requirements. When any event on the critical path slips beyond its expected date of accomplishment, it can also be expected that the final event will slip a similar amount.

*Slack and probabilities.* The first step in calculating slack and probabilities is to translate the engineers' estimates into measures descriptive of the mean time ($t_e$) and the uncertainty involved in that expectation, or the measure of its potential variability ($\sigma t_e^2$) for each activity by use of the following equations:

1. Mean times ($t_e$) are calculated for each activity by use of the following formula:

$$t_e = \frac{a + 4m + b}{6}$$

2.  The standard deviation is a measure of the uncertainty of an estimate. The variance for the range of distributions to be encountered is calculated for each activity by the formula:

$$\sigma\, t_e{}^2 = \left(\frac{b\text{-}a}{6}\right)^2$$

When a variance is small, the indication is that the estimates are fairly precise with little uncertainty, while a large variance indicates a great uncertainty on events accomplished. Small variances occur when the optimistic and pessimistic times are closest together.

3.  The expected time ($T_E$) for each event in the network is calculated by summing all the mean-time values for each activity along each series path in the network in order to obtain the elapsed time for selecting the path that requires the greatest amount of time to complete the end objective.

4.  The allowed time ($T_L$) and each event in the network are calculated by setting the $T_L$ of the end objective event as being equal to $T_E$ for the same event and computing backwards through the network to the base line or starting event by subtracting the mean time for each activity along each series path in the network related to applicable event.

5.  The probability associated with a schedule date ($T_S$) is calculated by use of the formula:

$$Z = \frac{T_S - T_E}{\sigma\, T_E}$$

At IBM, probabilities between 0.4 and 0.65 are considered the borderlines of reasonable risk and resource utilization. When probabilities are below 0.3, the danger is too great that the schedule will be missed and replanning is required. Probabilities between 0.3 and 0.4 require close scrutiny. When probabilities are above 0.65, resources for the defining path are excessive and replanning should be considered.

STEP 7: ANALYSIS AND EVALUATION

Computer output sheets are analyzed and evaluated to determine the most effective plan for doing the work in the shortest possible time. An attempt is made to achieve zero slack for all critical paths for each system, subsystem, equipment, and so forth. Each follows these basic steps:

1. Check information on computer output sheets for validity.
2. Analyze computer output sheets to make one or more of the following decisions:
   *a.* To replan portions of the network.
   *b.* To take early corrective action along the critical paths.
   *c.* To notify the prime contractor when schedule dates cannot be met.
   *d.* To request greater subcontract effort.
   *e.* To shift or add resources to comply with the network plan.
   *f.* To consider the application of overtime.
   *g.* To take on the risk of eliminating portions of the work.
   *h.* To consider the probability of meeting the schedule dates.

STEP 8: REPORTING

We have special reports to depict program status for top management, which needs valid and timely data on matters influencing the company's present position and matters which can be expected to influence this position in the future. In order to update PERT information continuously, managers are required to report the status of all events that have been completed or scheduled for completion and submit new elapsed-time estimates from a time-now base line for those activities that are currently being worked on for the next reporting period. The department manager also reports future events that appear to be in jeopardy by submitting new elapsed-time estimates. The monthly report calls for specific re-estimates for those events on critical paths as determined by the previous computer analysis and for critical events on positive slack paths. When an end-objective date is too far to the right of the manager's scheduled date, replanning decisions are made in regard to assuming greater technical risk and paralleling network efforts.

*Schedules.* From the PERT computer printouts, we are able to obtain a schedule for accomplishing work tasks. There should be but one schedule, and this schedule should depict the information listed on computer printouts. It is our intention that the PERT technique at IBM be utilized to its fullest capability, not just as a management tool but also as an engineering tool to achieve the best possible design within the schedule for each weapon system for which we have a design or project responsibility. PERT networks must not only reflect the planned schedule of milestone events, but also, by their very nature, include the capability of the facility to adhere to these milestones.

*Line of balance.* In addition to the PERT technique, we also use the line of balance technique. This technique is a methodical system for measuring, selecting, interpreting, and presenting facts in the manufacturing stages of an end item. It is a programing technique for measuring current progress against planned objectives—that is, where the program is in respect to where it should be. It employs the principle of exception, dealing only with the principal factors of a program and presents deviations from the plan. By the use of PERT, we evaluate the production performance of the first engineering models, from which we obtain a standard manufacturing plan and standard manufacturing times to be used in line of balance charts.

\* \* \*

It must be remembered that PERT Phase I (the time estimates) is not a complete planning and evaluation system or control system. When PERT Phase I is extended to include Phase II (adding manpower to get a more realistic and accurate projection of manpower requirements) and Phase III (adding money to get a more realistic and accurate projection of money flow and requirements for both labor and hardware), PERT will have great value as a simulation tool. Properly implemented, maintained, and analyzed, PERT offers management a means by which it is possible to analyze program status, determine bottlenecks, and use manpower effectively. The constant review of the objective, the plan to achieve the objective, the progress against the plan, and the necessary corrective action add up to good management coordination.

# USING PERT FOR CONTRACT ADMINISTRATION •

AUSTIN McHUGH

THERE ARE TWO types of contract administrators who use PERT in General Electric's Defense Systems Department (DSD): the marketing contract administrator and the procurement subcontract administrator. The marketing administrator oversees prime contracts or associate contracts from military customers. These are known as first-tier contracts. Our procurement administrator handles contracts between DSD and suppliers for goods and services (including the purchase of technology). These transactions are called second-tier subcontracts.

The PERTing activities of both these administrators are comprised of three phases: (1) preproposal and proposal, (2) contract award and definitization, and (3) implementation. The preproposal and proposal phase is that element of time when a request for proposal is anticipated before actual receipt of a document and that time which follows until the quotation is received by the soliciting agency. The contract award and definitization phase is that period of time when the customer evaluates potential bidders, selects the contractor, and negotiates items of the work with the awardee. The implementation phase is that time when the contractor has the right to proceed; it continues until the contract is completed.

PREPROPOSAL AND PROPOSAL PHASE

PERT is used by the marketing contract administrator early in marketing planning—during the preproposal and proposal phase. At DSD we have endeavored to capitalize on the *newness* of PERT and have applied it where we could derive the most planning and integrating

---

AUSTIN McHUGH is Manager, Producibility Engineering, Defense Systems Department, General Electric Company, Syracuse, New York.

*114*

benefits. We started using PERT in all new major program-proposal efforts in support of the marketing contract administrator. Our approach was unique because it applied a detailed planning technique to a relatively new environment. Almost immediately we began bucking years of ingrained proposal procedure.

Those who have worked on proposal teams have an idea of the amount of confusion that prevails during this period. They can appreciate the need for precise communication and confident direction for the preparation of a document that has a sacred customer deadline. They can visualize the gathering of company experts from all parts of the country (the majority of whom have never met before and are unaware of each other's capabilities) to resolve technical problems, write words for the proposal book, and prepare estimates of cost. These are the tools that the proposal leader must use to write the book.

It was precisely this book writing that we wanted to de-emphasize. We felt from earlier proposal ventures that there was entirely too much emphasis being placed upon writing for the customer. We further felt that, with the proper and timely introduction of a planning technique, we could mold company experts into a team by imparting total program knowledge. These team members, with the help of PERT, would then be in a position to resolve their interrelated problems with the balanced best interest of the program as their paramount objective. We did just what we set out to do, but it took approximately two years to install PERT thinking in the proposal phase and to divert the major effort of proposal teams from *writing* to *planning*. We cannot take full credit for PERTing proposals because the military services had already started asking contractors to provide, as part of the bid package, a network to demonstrate capability and program understanding.

We have been submitting detailed milestone plans in our proposals since 1958—changing to PERT early in 1960. Today some of the networks illustrated in our proposal brochures have as many as 1,600 to 1,800 activities and are accompanied by pages of computer printout and network analysis showing anticipated problem areas and recommended corrective action. In many cases during a proposal effort we have refined program networks eight or nine times on a computer before freezing the plan. In some instances we have PERTed the proposal activity to guarantee that a customer deadline will be met. Incidentally, this is one means of controlling proposal cost at DSD. As a result of our planning efforts, we have proved that our basic assumption holds true: that it is possible for the book to crystallize problems much quicker and exhibit a greater understanding, depth, and breadth of knowledge if people will *first* take the time to detail the proposed work graphically.

It can be said that the proposal book is simply a dissertation on the recommended approach—a book which tells *how, when,* and *how much.* PERT can help write this book, since it includes a narrative of how we intend to accomplish the mission. Thus the book is essentially a verbal description of the PERT plan and amplifies the technology involved. Just as the PERT network can help develop the words for the proposal text, it can also help save valuable words. PERT planning has particular merit if the proposal has a word limitation; the network illustrations can substitute successfully for narrative.

Usually the book discusses the extent of pure and applied research for advances in systems technology. PERT can assist by calculating available time for "pushing the state of the art" or for selecting off-the-shelf items by weighing all program time elements simultaneously to arrive at the realistic *when* value of each. There may not be time for design; off-the-shelf items may be all that time will allow. PERT will indicate this clearly.

Just as PERT can help write the book, it can also help determine the cost. The cost summary submitted as part of the proposal is nothing more than a tabulation of the work activities denoting *how much.* It is expressed in dollars of manpower, materials, and resources required to implement the recommended approach. The PERT network is a graphic summary of work activities expressed in time and therefore a valuable transposing mechanism for determining items of cost.

*Marketing.* The life of a proposal effort is generally around 30 days; this is an extremely short period of time. DSD has been using the PERT system with our marketing contract administrators during the preproposal phase—or that time when we await delivery of a customer's request for proposal—to buy time or extend the proposal phase. It is well recognized that the more time we have to work on a proposal, the more significant decreases we should be able to make in the over-all cost and the more concrete our recommendations will be.

By taking this approach, DSD accepts a certain amount of risk, since we have no more information about the system than any other potential bidder. Essentially, we gamble by anticipating customer requirements, and we assume that the work statement will be written in a manner sufficiently broad and flexible to permit ingenuity and creativity on our part to resolve the problem. Historically, in our type of business, the majority of requests for proposals are written in this fashion. Undoubtedly some elements of work will change. Yet we are much better off factoring in changes to our plan and levying decisions on interface problems with the unchanged portion of the plan than we are starting cold with a customer's request for proposal (RFP) and a proposal group made up of strangers. We have, in effect, bought valuable, unmeasurable proposal time if we only reduce the time it will take for each team member to learn and understand the RFP.

Experience has taught us that in order to plan effectively in advance of a customer RFP, we require three planning aids to PERT:

1.  A model RFP—commonly called a dummy work statement.
2.  Standard PERT networks or generalized functional networks.
3.  A system-planning model, which is a glossary of work activities.

These have all been developed and are in use, effectively reducing the cost of DSD proposal activity.

During the preproposal phase of an unsolicited bid, PERT networks help fill a gap in communications between the customer and the marketing contract administrator. Some of our marketing administrators are sufficiently schooled to use PERT networks as a "talking paper." If they are not, PERT planners can accompany them to the customer's house. The use of a network at this time allows an exchange of ideas in a format that leaves little to imagination or interpretation. It is an understandable, permanent reference for both the marketing man and the customer. This working network, when brought back to us, provides an excellent base from which to disseminate information to engineering, manufacturing, and field service personnel and is the foundation for more detailed planning. The customer will also find value in using his copy of the network to discuss pertinent problems with his superiors or other government experts. It may travel back and forth between the customer and DSD many times before it matures sufficiently for either party to take action. When the action results in an oral presentation, the network makes an excellent illustration for exchange of information. When the action results in a solicited or unsolicited proposal, the network becomes the backbone of proposal planning.

*Procurement.* Large systems preproposal and proposal activities involve contact with many industrial enterprises. It is at these interfaces that the procurement subcontract administrator plays a major role with our suppliers. We PERT not only internal DSD functions for the fielding of a complex system but the DSD *potential* subcontract program as well. We learned a long time ago that in order to commit a complex systems program plan to paper in a factual manner, joint PERTing efforts are required of all associate contractors and suppliers during or prior to proposal activity. We cannot plan a system and "guesstimate" the subcontractor program, because the subcontract portion is a major part of our business.

During formal bidding, our potential suppliers are requested to submit networks along with the usual technical data and cost information. Procurement subcontract administrators or buyers prepare quote packages which include a simple PERT planning specification and a simple report specification, each four to five pages in length. Since they are written in this fashion, we reduce the scare factor associated with a new or unknown specification and thus minimize the factor of "so many dollars per pound or inch of specification" which sneaks into quotations as protection against the unknown. In addition, the potential supplier receives a small brochure, written in the language of the supplier, which explains PERT. There is no need for the supplier to search for supporting data: sufficient information is contained in the brochure to teach him how to prepare a network. In fact, a sample network of some 60 events appears in the booklet to assist the supplier in deciding how much detail and depth of programing are required.

The buyer decides whether this specification will be included in the bid package. It is placed only on those subcontracts that are significantly high in dollar value, crucial in schedule, or "pushing the state of the art." The types of contracts make little difference. Some purchases will require simple networks while others will be quite extensive. Remember, we are only asking him to convert his planning into PERT format at a level of detail which will permit program assessment and, in turn, provide him with program information in sufficient detail to assist him. We still include milestone and line of balance planning and reporting specifications in bid packages where applicable.

As soon as the supplier's network is received at DSD, it is fitted into the total program network. Then our computer tells us when the critical path goes through the subcontract program. If we find the critical path objectionable in a particular subsystem network, the buyer contacts the concerned suppliers, states the subsystem's effect on the total program, and requests corrective action. This change may entail a requote or a change in the total program plan.

Two years ago we thought it would be extremely difficult for us to PERT the subcontract program during the preproposal and proposal phase. Taking the time to educate our suppliers, we found that it could be done during this hectic period because the suppliers felt they were getting something out of it. DSD can show no partiality when instructing suppliers during the proposal phase.

CONTRACT AWARD AND DEFINITIZATION PHASE

*Marketing.* DSD, its potential associates, and its suppliers are now thinking PERT because of our pioneering in the preproposal and proposal phase. If the contract is awarded to us, we have established the knowledge base and rapport for the definitization phase with respect to dealing with the customer and our suppliers as well as internally within DSD functions.

Assuming that the customer has evaluated all proposals and has decided who will be awarded the contract, he will undoubtedly know more about the job at hand and more about the funds required—as a result of his comprehensive analysis of all the proposals submitted. At this point, the task of definitizing the contract is in the hands of the marketing contract administrator and the customer. Definitization basically involves determining and agreeing on at least three criteria for each item of the work statement: the target dates (time) to produce a qualifying end item to the system (specification) at a cost (dollars).

Marketing can now refer to the PERT plan submitted in the proposal, which represents our interpretation of each item of the proposal work statement, and negotiate for time, specifications, and dollars for each item of the contractual work statement. As a result, an improved network will be generated to capture the best of associated ideas, scope changes, and trade-offs, all of which is done in a customer-oriented format where little is lost in translation. This network satisfies the customer and DSD. We now have a mutually envisioned plan which denotes what work elements we will do and, conversely and indirectly, what work elements we will not do.

We must next examine the network to determine whether costs reflect planned effort. PERT network elements are comprised of work tasks which are definable in terms of manpower, materials, and resources. Work tasks can be summarized for each item of the contract and expressed in dollars. Therefore, the network represents the plan for accomplishment of a job with planned hours of manpower, planned materials, and planned usage of resources.

However, up till now the network has been used for planning purposes only, each element being expressed in time. For costing purposes each element of the network can also be expressed in manpower, materials, and resources, which can be converted into dollars. Tabulation of these dollars represents, in essence, contract cost. We have been singing the praises of PERT as a planning tool—that is, a device which improves the knowlege base and so forth and soon. Many people have been sitting back and awaiting the development of the PERT/Cost technique and have not investigated or applied the potential of PERT/-Time as a costing tool—a device which improves the cost base.

In our business, where we spearhead in the field of technological breakthroughs, manpower is our biggest element of cost. Our ability to quote competitively and perform for the quote is enhanced by continuous emphasis on effective utilization of our manpower. Axiomatically, plans are people, and people are cost. Therefore, plans control people and people control cost. DSD is using the cost potential of PERT in its present form at a very crucial time—the contract award and definitization phase—to support the cost proposal. The application of PERT during this phase is improving our ability to be on time, on cost, and on specification.

*Procurement.* When the prime contract has been awarded, we must assess and select the required subcontractors from the potential vendors and suppliers who participated with us during the bid phase, just as the military selected DSD from other potential prime contractors. The procurement subcontract administrator is charged with this responsibility. He utilizes technical experts and business analysis to assist him in making this decision. One of the tools he uses is the PERT plan.

During the bid phase, we request potential suppliers to demonstrate their capabilities uniformly by requesting the preparation of a PERT plan. We use the network as one criterion of assessment to determine just how well the vendor comprehends the job; it may become necessary to send a survey team to the vendor's plant to conduct this assessment. If so, the network accompanies the team and is instrumental in determining whether a supplier has the necessary manpower, tools, facilities, and know-how to do the job.

When DSD has made the selection of its subcontractors, PERT plans developed by the suppliers contribute to definitizing contracts with our suppliers in a way similar to our use of networks to definitize with the military customer. Once the definitized network is agreed upon, it becomes the approved plan to guide both procurement and the supplier.

It is interesting that only significant milestones or key events are negotiated as contractual agreements. If the supplier must deviate from any one of these contractual key events, it must be with our concurrence. Often our agreement alone is insufficient and cannot be given without the consent of our customer, who is holding us to customer key events which may be affected. However, we do not hold our suppliers to all events appearing in a network. If all events were made contractual, then the supplier would not have the flexibility needed to make "in house" adjustments, and the network would lose its effectiveness as a working agreement. This mutually agreed-upon PERT plan between DSD and the supplier becomes the foundation for cost considerations just as the mutually agreed-upon network between DSD and the military customer formed the basis for cost.

We assume good planning from our suppliers and respect their integrity regardless of the planning system which the supplier uses. We only ask our suppliers to furnish us with an "intelligent cut" of planning which is sufficient in depth and detail on a PERT format so that we can successfully interface with other suppliers and our military customer. If a supplier wants to adopt the PERT system internally, that is the supplier's business. It is probable that if the supplier does change, it will be for the same reason that DSD changed: PERT provided us with a better system of planning, integrating, and measuring than we had previously known.

IMPLEMENTATION PHASE

*Marketing.* We had a very interesting experience the first time that the evaluation and review features of programing were used with the customer. Our programing knowledge was acquired through an excellent association with the Special Projects Office of the Navy. The project to which we first applied programing techniques was in the implementation phase and under an Air Force contract. Our marketing contract administrator was responsible for reporting status to the customer. At one monthly meeting, programing specialists participated with marketing personnel to make the presentation for the Air Force. Slides and publications were designed which used the new programing format. We fully expected to devote considerable time at the beginning of the meeting to an explanation of our new and exotic technique. Much to our surprise, no difficulty was experienced at all—the Air Force was well versed in our "unique" approach.

For reporting, either orally or in writing, at the customer level or internally within DSD, we keep the graphic illustrations very simple. Status and prediction data are concise and chronological; therefore, they are related to previous reports. The amount of report detail is entirely dependent on the audience. We report according to each item of the contract, depicting each item on a network of 10 to 20 events. These broad top-level networks are developed by combining and generalizing the more detailed work networks and by designing them specifically to satisfy the needs of the management level being reported to. We report entirely by the exception principle—that is, we report *only* problem areas; therefore, management can assume that those items not mentioned are not in trouble and that trouble is not contemplated. When a problem area is reported, it is accompanied by recommended courses of action. Sometimes explanations or feedback appear in reports to keep management aware of problems resolved through authority delegated to lower levels of management. The degree of criticalness of a problem decides the level of report that it will appear in; this may very well be determined by the degree of authority required to break the bottleneck. For example, the procurement subcontract administrator must increase the production rate of a "black box" in a supplier's shop or miss a delivery date which is critical. The situation involves an increase in tooling cost, and the authorization for the expenditure is reserved by the project maanger. Therefore, this action requires the administrator's approval and appears in the report to the project manager.

*Procurement.* Let us examine how DSD's buyer arrived at the decision to request an increase in tooling cost for the black-box supplier through the use of a PERT network. Historically, procurement has purchased cabinets, subsystems, and systems by means of engineering work statements. There is no question whether the procurement people know the mechanics of subcontracting (the administrative function, funding procedures, and government regulations), nor is the ability to work with the supplier in doubt. The question is whether the procurement function has sufficient timely information available from suppliers to make the right decision from a total program prospective. The buyer has always depended upon the engineer to aid him, with respect to work-statement content. Because of the buyer's background, he probably always will rely technically on the engineer, but PERT plans help him understand more about the work statement by logically and graphically portraying the approach needed to accomplish each item of work.

At any point in time, the buyer can review the plan with the supplier. The interval for formal reporting or formal review is based on a frequency that is sufficient to monitor. Normally, this time period varies from two to four weeks, although more frequent formal reviews may be necessary at a time of crisis. In any event, the buyer—with the aid of the PERT plan—can now accomplish the following: (1) challenge contractual events in the progress of work; (2) monitor the progress of suppliers through the engineering phase as well as other phases, because PERT is prepared in a layman's language; (3) ask intelligent questions by referring to the proper terminology in the network; and (4) use PERT to predict outcome rather than rely on some intuitive assurance that the supplier *may* meet a target date.

In the case of the supplier who was in need of additional funds for increased tool cost, the buyer—with the aid of PERT—did the following: (1) asked the DSD computer to determine what effect supplier slippage would have on the total program; (2) requested trial recycling in other areas, which would result in a less costly change; (3) consider recommending authorization to extend to a new target date with sufficient program information to explain this change convincingly to the supplier; and (4) recommend intelligently the authorization of additional funds, based on program facts. We are now breeding this kind of buyer, who no longer needs to fly by the seat of his pants.

THE POTENTIAL OF PERT

DSD has not reached a utopian plateau with PERT, nor is it now operating a completely stable programing system: we have a long way to go before we gain the full potential of PERT. Merely to institute PERT thinking at the marketing and procurement interfaces and get a toe hold in the phases mentioned, we began with a soft-sell program in 1960. It has required the patience of approximately a dozen PERT experts, strategically placed in the engineering, manufacturing, and field service organizations. The task of educating did not start with the marketing and procurement people: it began with the people who provide input to the networks—the specialists. Every business opportunity was utilized to instill PERT thinking, and planning and integrating gradually improved. Today we hasten this learning procedure somewhat by conducting formal PERT courses, with the emphasis on military-systems planning.

We recognized back in 1958 that the major problem would involve "the creative individual." Our people are primarily technological specialists in a broad spectrum of disciplines. This age of specialists in which we work has given us people very narrow in outlook, highly skilled in a particular field but having very little appreciation of the other tasks involved in fielding a major military system and a limited understanding of the over-all project. Today we have an urgent need in our industry for personnel who take an interest in the total project while solving their own problems—men who can look at a task through the eyes of engineering, manufacturing, finance, and field service as well as through those of their prime specialties. PERT is helping us to develop these generalists.

It has been our objective to help the specialists become aware of the tremendous potential of PERT. We assist them in taking advantage of the sales value in the logic of the PERT scheme, which often intrigues engineers. We capitalized on this, and gradually, over a period of time, specialists realized PERT's value to themselves. We walked slowly and followed a PERT sales program that was specifically designed to suit our environment. PERT sold itself. All we had to do was create the atmosphere, provide the impetus, and remember that it would not take hold overnight.

# PRACTICAL ADVICE FOR THE USE
# OF PERT •

HAROLD G. FRANCIS

---

A S EVERY NEW TECHNIQUE or area of human endeavor makes its
appearance, there always arises a certain amount of specialized terminology. This generally comes about because it is easier to generate new
words than to use old ones and perhaps because it enables those who
first come on the scene to make others think something magical or
difficult is involved.

PERT is no exception to this phenomenon. Enough PERT jargon has
been developed to confuse and scare many people. However, PERT—
especially basic PERT—is really an easy concept to understand.
Knowledge about PERT is picked up quite rapidly, but, of course, real
skill in PERTing comes only with experience. One cannot really know
how to PERT a job well—with all the necessary trade-offs and replanning that are involved—unless one has had actual practice in the
application of this technique.

However, some assistance can be gained from the experience of
others. We at General Electric would like to share what we have learned
with those who are interested in PERT. We would also like to suggest
some guidelines to follow and propose a list of do's and don'ts.

GUIDELINES FOR THE USE OF PERT

Many people wonder exactly where PERT can be used. They ask
whether it is better on small jobs or big jobs. The answer is that there
is no restriction on the size of the project. My company has used
PERT on small development jobs of $10,000 and less as well as on

---

HAROLD G. FRANCIS is Manager, Detectional Surveillance Products Engineering,
Light Military Electronics Department, Defense Electronics Division, General
Electric Company, Utica, New York.

multimillion-dollar programs. It has helped us at both ends of the scale.

In every organization, a training program will have to be set up to implement PERT. We at General Electric started out by selling the system to individual workers and managers up the line. We did this by PERT briefings which we gave at any and all meetings at any organizational level to which we could get ourselves invited. In each case we geared our PERT orientation to the level of the individuals in the particular groups. In order for PERT to be used fully, personnel throughout the organization must understand and know how to use the system. We prepared a detailed training course for these people. The course lasted five days, and each day's session lasted for two and a half hours and included homework. Approximately a hundred people went through the course. We reached our present level of PERT efficiency in the period immediately following the completion of these training courses. Progress in implementation was much more rapid and less argumentative after this.

The PERT consultants or planners in our organization are all engineers since all of our work is highly technical. We consider these people to be protagonists or devil's advocates. They do not actually do the planning when they are in the PERT sessions because *those doing the work* must, of course, make their own plans. However, they know what questions to ask to uncover the soft spots. By knowing other jobs going through the plant and the difficulties encountered, they know what to look for and what to avoid. We often find that the PERT consultants convey this type of information from one project to another and save considerable time and money. This communication is an extra gain from PERT and is another argument for using people who are technically oriented.

We always teach our PERT consultants to do completed staff work, which is no different in PERT than it is in any other type of activity. We believe in taking solutions to the problems shown by PERT to the managers. It only delays the solution if we wait for a manager to analyze the problem. When the consultant goes to a manager, he should tell him the alternatives so that the manager can then make the decision.

In our department in Utica, we have three separate plants. At each of these locations we have established what we call a "PERTatorium." These are conference rooms set aside for the PERTing of projects. They have no calendars on the walls, no telephones, but do have plenty of blackboard and chart space. By isolating people from their work, we found that they could do a better and faster job on planning with PERT. The absence of the calendar produced better time estimates because it forced them to think of the work and not just of the schedule.

We have gotten the greatest benefit from PERT when we have kept the networks simple—that is, the networks should be made on vellum paper, in pencil, and not by a draftsman. In no case should networks be inked, unless they are needed for reproduction purposes in a proposal or some other publication.

It is possible to do some of the calculations in PERT by hand. We do have a nomograph that we use on some occasions. As experience in PERT grows, it is possible to make these calculations rapidly. However, it does get to be a boring part of the job. In general, hand calculations are not used unless there is an emergency or the network is so small that it is wasteful to go to the computer.

The question of how long it takes to PERT a job is difficult to answer unless one knows the depth of the planning that is required. Our standard, however, has been two hours per 100 events with about one of the two hours spent on decision making. This applies to the initial network when those participating have some knowledge of PERT. A PERTing session should, as a general rule, not last over three or four hours in one day. This is about all that a group can do without becoming sloppy. Besides, this time limit holds a network to about 300 events, which is the recommended size when possible.

It is best to get back with an analysis to the people making the plan no more than two days later and preferably within 24 hours. If we do not get back to them rapidly, their interest generally diminishes, their confidence wanes, and the time for the decision passes.

The amount of detail required is another question that frequently arises. How small a work content or short a time should the activities on the networks have? We can consider that we have planned to the proper depth when we are able to get adequate warning of difficulties that will occur in the future. We should go into whatever detail is necessary to understand the full significance of the activity. If the detail is excessive, however, we will find that we are not getting a true prediction. The only real way to find out is to PERT a few jobs and get a feel for it. There are no hard and fast rules.

One point often overlooked by those learning the PERT technique is that the activity between two events can be broken down into a complete, separate network. If we spot an area that is critical or that looks strange for some reason or another, it is best to make a separate network for it.

As far as the minimum time is concerned, it is better to use weeks than days; but sometimes, when trouble is really at hand, using days may be necessary. We must remember that a number of people working a short time get paid as much as a few people working for a long time.

Engineering often gets committed to release a job on a specific date and must release it regardless of the need for total release by the manufacturing groups. We have found that PERT planning has greatly increased understanding between engineering and manufacturing. When we release a job, we are able to release the items piecemeal as needed by manufacturing and determined by PERT. As long as the manufacturing people understand the over-all sequence of releases, it does not bother them. They no longer scream for engineering to release unless we are really at fault. Better understanding and better relations with manufacturing save time, arguing, and money and keep the inventory low.

A LIST OF DO'S

1. *Get top management support.* One thing that can never be minimized in the implementing of a PERT system is top management support. It is generally agreed by all who have used PERT that this is mandatory. However, by support we mean *encouragement* and not commands. Arbitrary imposition of PERT will hinder its eventual acceptance. This is true even though resistance to PERT is now weaker than it used to be. In fact, PERT is coming into such widespread use that people are becoming afraid *not* to use it.

2. *Adapt PERT to local requirements.* Every plant is different, and each has its own peculiar organization. Within General Electric, departments are organized exactly alike; but the people are different, the businesses are different, and the PERT needs are different.

3. *Replan when necessary.* One of the basic features of the PERT technique is that replanning is inherent. We first plan the project ideally and then make the necessary changes to get within the prescribed schedule limitations. There have been instances in which PERT

systems have been set up where the plans required formal alteration notices and formal meetings to get them changed. In other cases the networks were frozen and never changed. Such procedures are considered to be too rigid and time-consuming and are generally bad practice. If at any time new difficulties arise which call for a change in the PERT planning, we should make the change and go on from there.

With PERT we are taking advantage of the laws of probability. Even though one event might be missed, we can very well pick up the time on another one; and if we do not, we can replan later events. Many people forget this and panic too quickly.

On the other hand, it is sometimes overlooked that replanning in PERT inherently increases the risk of not meeting a schedule. The first plan and the first time estimates for a job usually are found to be best. We should not change the estimates once they are made unless the plans are changed. However, in planning alternatives, we must be sure to consider the increase in risk that follows.

4. *Leave room for expansion.* When we set up a PERT system, we must be sure to set it up so that it can grow and expand as time progresses. We cannot install a PERT system with high-caliber people and then leave it for lower-level people to operate. We should always have some knowledgeable individual working with PERT and adapting it to newer requirements. Moreover, the system should not be frozen after it gets working properly. When installing it, we should indicate to the users that it will change from time to time. Like all systems, PERT should be flexible and changed to meet the needs of the users when this is desirable and necessary.

5. *Establish PERT on a permanent basis.* Since PERT has now become a contractual requirement for most military customers, some PERT systems have been set up just to satisfy the customer. This may accomplish its aim in the short run, but in the long run the customer will find it out. Furthermore, to use PERT just to keep the customer happy is like keeping the front parlor locked up for use only when visitors come.

A LIST OF DON'TS

1. *Don't force formal reporting.* We have for a long time steadfastly maintained that PERT is basically a *planning* tool which will

report what we want it to. In implementing a PERT operation, some may find that they only want the work planned and do not want any formal reporting back to management. This is as it should be. We should not force formal reporting into a PERT system unless there is a real need for it. When reports *are* necessary, they should be geared to the information requirements of each level involved.

Much of the success of PERT has been attributed to the fact that it just does not take the information, chew it up, and then send it back and pretend as if it were something new. PERT *adds* new information.

2. *Don't use inaccurate estimates.* We can lie to PERT as easily as we can to any other system. But if we do, we will only be wasting time and money. There have been cases where PERT groups have been fed spurious data for parts of a job. This is obvious when the whole job is analyzed. Excessively long estimates will show up on the critical path. There is nothing wrong about being on the critical path: somebody has to be there. However, if we show up there all the time, there is usually something wrong. The effect of a safe estimate is to force management to take increased risks in other areas. Being accurate with PERT estimates pays off.

3. *Don't add time estimates first.* In planning a project with PERT, we should first plan the network and then add time estimates. These should be made at random. If we start estimating at one end of the network and work our way through, we will probably pick up the possible critical paths and shorten the estimates on these paths. The randomizing of the time estimating eliminates this difficulty.

4. *Don't demand commitments.* One point which cannot be over-stressed is that we must be sure to separate our estimates from our commitments. An estimate is an estimate and not a commitment. We should use commitments only when absolutely necessary. We must realize that a man is exercising his best judgment, when he gives us estimates, and we should not force him to a commitment. If we do, we will get longer estimates the next time.

5. *Don't plan with overtime.* When planning with PERT the first time through, estimates should be based on a normal workweek, and overtime should be saved for schedule completion when needed. Other-wise this method of shortening the schedule is lost later on when it is needed for handling trouble spots.

6. *Don't standardize event titles.* One other pitfall to avoid is standardizing event titles. We all agree that standardization is necessary for many facets of our work. In PERT, however, standardization of event titles tends to slow planning and cause confusion. At first, we made this mistake. We compiled a list of event titles and tried to get everyone to use them. We found that the people doing the planning spent more time deciding on which event title should be used than they did on planning. We decided to let those doing the work call the events what they wished. This worked out very well because then it was *their* plan of *their* work. What is important is that those doing the work agree on and understand the terms they use.

# RESEARCH IN PERT METHODS AND TECHNOLOGY •

G. TRUMAN HUNTER

---

THE FEDERAL SYSTEMS DIVISION of IBM has been using PERT procedures for some time. During this period separate research efforts have been under way to advance the basic PERT technology. The following topics have been studied: the addition of resources (direct labor and costs) to the basic time-only PERT procedures, a study of the validity of the three time estimates compared to actual performance, data-processing procedures which may assist in PERT processing, and the ability to have PERT networks printed automatically by a computer.

ADDITION OF RESOURCES TO TIME-ONLY PERT

All locations of the Federal Systems Division (FSD) have procedures for processing information for management control purposes. These were prepared and have been improved so that IBM could have the best possible management control of projects. A group is now working at one of the FSD manufacturing locations to implement the concepts of linking PERT with present reporting and accounting systems to get an even more powerful management information system. The aim is to disturb each basic system as little as possible and to utilize its best features and concepts.

An obvious advantage can be gained by including manpower as part of the basic PERT information. Of course, additional programs will

---

G. TRUMAN HUNTER is Administrator, Educational Program, Data Processing Division, International Business Machines Corporation, White Plains, New York.

have to be written to retrieve and arrange this information. If the time to complete an activity can be estimated, some average number of men must have been assumed to be working during this period. Also, something must be known of the skills which these men must be using. Skills can be coded by means of present or new codes and included as basic data.

If manpower information is available for each activity and if a vertical cut is taken across a PERT network for a given time period, such as one week, it is then possible to find the total manpower required for all activities scheduled during that week. Variations of this information could provide totals by time, department, skill, or any combination of these.

Since PERT is a common language for all projects, it should be possible to sum up these requirements for several networks or projects. The total requirements could then be shown as a bar graph or histogram covering many time periods, and the computer could actually prepare these charts automatically. The total requirements could be compared to availability, and the excess or lack of manpower or skill could be shown as a function of time. This concept can be used for computer time, special test equipment, or any resource that people are willing to include in their planning as a distinct coded item.

A computer program developed by IBM and called LESS (Least Cost Estimating and Scheduling) is something like PERT. Only one time estimate is given for each activity. The program then computes a time schedule and finds the critical path and the various slack paths. A second part of the LESS program goes on to summarize the total number of men being used for all jobs in progress during each time period. A maximum of ten skills may be coded. The program will also reschedule activities (within slack limitations) where the number of men required exceeds the number of men available. A third part of the LESS program is being prepared which will allow schedule changes to be computed on the basis of the relationship between linear time and cost trade-off.

Once manpower is known, direct hours can be calculated by department or skill or both. The computer can then apply hourly rates to these hours to get direct labor charges. Burden rates can be applied in the usual accounting fashion to develop indirect labor and other charges. With each activity we can associate a materials estimate, subcontract expense, living expense, and any other of the usual general categories used in making up the ordinary project budget.

All of these procedures are accomplished today by some combination of hand and machine methods, but they have generally not been related to PERT. If the PERT network and data are assumed to be the best possible statement of work to be performed in connection with a project, they then should also be the basis for summaries of costs, manpower, skills, and other resources.

Thus, PERT can be modified to forecast the level of resources which will be required for the duration of the project. It should be understood, of course, that as new data are added and processed, the changes will be reflected over the entire project. However, this is only part of the information which is needed for controlling a project. Also required is the actual or project-to-date status.

Present FSD management information systems use weekly reporting intervals. By the middle of the following week, data-processing machines have printed a variety of reports at summary and detail levels which include man-hours, direct and indirect charges, some past as well as present information, and budget data. This is typical of what a good accounting installation can do. But up to now this information has not been related to PERT activity detail.

The present systems could easily report for all PERT projects, if each project had only 20 activities or so. Since, however, a PERT network on a good-sized project may have as many as 2,000 activities, the sudden demand to expand the accounting system by a factor of 100 is obviously a problem.

As we study the expansion of PERT and the printing of PERT networks, the key factor seems to be the determination of the proper size of a typical PERT activity. If a project is to last a couple of years and occupy dozens or hundreds of men at the same time, it hardly seems to make sense to ask for a complete schedule for every man for every day (although ultimately this information must be available). On the other hand, to ask for a report on 100 men only every three months or so would provide too little control. It would seem reasonable to ask for activities of one to four weeks' duration, with some exceptions allowed outside that range. For accounting purposes the system should allow for grouping some activities—probably in series rather than in parallel. This would permit a reduction in accounting classifications without much loss of detail and control. Summary networks used for reporting to top management must also group detail activities into much larger units to give a simple picture.

A special program will have to be prepared which can process actual information, produce reports of project progress to date, and then extend them into the future by using the forecast type of information, the latest burden rates, and so on to give project forecasts. Compromises will have to be made among the several interested parties. Accounting by tradition likes to give completely documented facts, and it takes time to get them in completed form. Project managers want up-to-date information and will trade some inaccuracy in approximations for current reporting. Accounting does not generally like to make forecasts, and yet top management needs them (with known limits of inaccuracy) for some time into the future in order to do long-range planning.

Reporting to the complete system may take the form of punched cards or lists prepared by a data-procesing machine so that a minimum of human reading, writing, and interpretation will be required. In longer-range thinking, reporting may be done via remote recording devices which are directly connected to a central processing machine.

Systems in the past have usually used account-number codes organized so that relatively simple sorting machines and procedures could isolate certain categories of information. Now that much more powerful machines and techniques are available for sorting and retrieving information—for example, the IBM KWIC (Key Word in Context) System—this coding restriction on a management information system has been decreased if not eliminated.

ADDITIONAL STUDIES UNDER WAY

One of the critical problems in the application of advanced techniques for management planning and control of R&D is the accuracy and variability of the data used. A first look at this problem has reached the final stage of investigation at the Systems Center. Experimental research has examined the individual and joint effects on the accuracy and variability of performance time estimates of (1) the line or staff management context within which estimates are made and (2) the level of definition of the work to be performed. Preliminary results indicate significant effects for these variables which, when interpreted in terms of techniques, should lead to improved quality in management input data.

Other projected studies at the Systems Center include the development of logical and mathematical models which interrelate performance variables such as cost and time. Methods are being considered for the construction of resource curves for the trade-off of time-effort and time-cost for R&D activities. Furthermore, the effects of the joint probability distribution for event completion time and cost are to be studied. Finally, research is being directed at the problem of multiple and competing R&D project resources requirements. Combinatorial techniques are to be developed for the aggregation of potential expenditures and the allocation of dollars and manpower to tasks for concurrent project development within the restraints of limited resources.

In order to help implement the processing of PERT information, some additions to the usual PERT programs have been written. A preprocessor-editor program has been written to do file maintenance of additions, changes, and deletions to the basic 7090 PERT program. Another program has been prepared to be merged with the first, and it will isolate loops and find loose ends so that these may be checked and corrected (if need be) before a PERT schedule is calculated. Still a third program will permit the printing of summary information from marked key events in the complete detail network.

One tool which has proved to be very useful is an activity listing, by event number, in which all the activities leading to and from each event are grouped together for easy reference. It has also been suggested that a historical file of activities, with both estimates and actual performance data, should be kept. It could be analyzed in many different ways so that past experience might help on future projects.

NETWORK PRINTOUT BY MACHINE

The first PERT network for a project is usually laid out on one or more sheets of paper. There is little if any organization with respect to calendar time and no knowledge of the critical path. After the first PERT machine run, time, and critical path information are available. It is usually a laborious assignment for a draftsman to redraw the PERT network in a more organized, readable, "cleaned up" form. Then, as often happens, within a few weeks or months many changes have been made in the plan of work. These are processed quickly by the PERT program, and the usual updated activity lists are printed. But to redraw the network requires a repeat of the drafting effort, which tends to increase as the square of the number of events in the network.

There are several approaches to simplifying the network-representation problem before getting to an actual machine procedure. If activities can be grouped together, it is possible to reduce the problem to what might be called a summary network. Obviously, a network of 50 events should be easier to handle than one of 500 events. Along with the gain in ease of handling, however, there is a loss of detail which may be acceptable to some people but not to others.

Another method is to maintain the network in sections—by department, component, or some other simple unit. This makes each sub-network easier to draw but does not give a picture of the over-all relationship of the activities to each other or with respect to time. If events are printed only as numbers, without the usual alphabetic, descriptive text and if the activity descriptions and times are left out, the network becomes easier to draw because of the lack of complicating (and supporting) detail. This detail, however, may be made available from a simple cross-reference list or even added by hand after the basic network has been printed.

*Problems of dimension.* Since a PERT network is printed on a piece of paper, it must be arranged in a two-dimensional manner. The horizontal dimension is usually time, which increases from left to right. The scale may be absolute time or relative time.

Absolute time as a scale tends to waste paper and may make the PERT network rather large. A three-year network, printed on a scale of six days to the inch, would occupy about 15 feet. This requires a good deal of wall space, but it does allow observation of times to the nearest day if this is desired.

Relative time allows the time scale to be condensed when there are no events to be printed. This saves paper but makes the accurate comparison of activity duration impossible. It may also require the expansion of zero-time activities, which reduces previous savings and makes time comparisons even less meaningful.

The vertical dimension is the more difficult of the two to work out for the PERT network. There are several different sorts of sequences or logics which could be used to arrange the activities. Each one of these violates most or all of the others:

1. Arrangement by event or activity number is of no use because it would greatly complicate the initial numbering system.
2. Arranging activities by slack paths is not very satisfactory because it tends to separate paths with common end points.
3. Grouping slack paths by common starting or ending events tends to confuse the picture more than it helps for any but truly parallel branch paths.
4. Sorting paths by time lengths, time of starting, or time of ending tends to spoil other patterns.

Some projects, by their nature, may be such that one of these ideas furnishes a specific solution. Others may require the critical path to be in the center of the network, with the rest placed symmetrically about it. This is a very neat arrangement, but it is often difficult to achieve.

*A possible solution.* There is a solution which seems to fit a rather general class of network. First, if a project divides naturally into parallel sections, the network can be divided into subnetworks which can be placed side by side with a minimum of cross connections. Next, the network is constructed in terms of individual slack paths. Each slack path is a logical sequence of activities ending in a milestone event which is usually on another path of less slack.

The characteristics of the IBM 1403, which was chosen for the printing process, are such that it is much easier for the machine to draw straight lines either horizontally or vertically than to draw lines at any angle or to draw curves. The resulting network will be somewhat stylized and restricted in comparison to the usual networks drawn by hand. Actually, it resembles a Gantt chart with certain specific rules for positioning each of the horizontal bars in the vertical dimension.

The horizontal axis of the network is time. The vertical axis has no specific scale; it is used merely to separate the several activities which are going on simultaneously. Two activities which end in the same event will show up as two adjacent parallel lines, each ending in the identical event number and on the same date. In other words, the usual single event number has spread out vertically in paper space to touch both activity lines. If eight or ten activities should end in the same event number, that number will be printed eight or ten times— once at the end of each appropriate activity. These printings all occur at the same date on the time scale, so it is easy to find the multiple printings. Another event may also appear at the same time, but it will have a different event number. The several events with different numbers all occurring at the same time can be arranged in increasing number sequence. (They can be separately marked in color or distinguished by hand in some other fashion.)

To sum up, all activities representing project work to be done lie parallel to the horizontal time axis. Dummy or no-time activities needed for logical processing of the network would also be included. Vertical axis lines would be used only when necessary to connect the several activities ending in a common event.

Where a dummy or no-time activity is used, it will result in two event numbers in the same path appearing on the same date. In this case, the second event must be pushed to the next later printing position and marked with an asterisk to show that it has been printed out of position. It is never placed at the side of a path where it might interfere with events on another path.

In general, the time scale for the network should be chosen so that most activities occupy at least one time unit (except for dummy or no-time activities). If the unit is one day, activities should be at least one day long. If the time unit is half a week, then the activities should be at least as long as half a week. The critical path is placed at the bottom of the net, next to the time scale. All other paths are arranged above the critical path.

The parallel path positions are called fields. If six-digit positions are allowed in each field, then 20 fields can be printed at one time, along with the time scale, on a sheet of paper 14 inches wide (between sprocket holes). If two or more subpaths end on the same path at different times (different events), they should be arranged by increasing end date, the earliest in the field closest to the final path. If two slack paths do not overlap in time, they may be printed in the same field. For example, if one slack path occupies the month of March and another the month of May, they can both be printed in the same field. However, if one path occupies the months of March and April and a second path the months of April and May, they must be placed in separate fields so that they do not overlap. If two or more subpaths end at the same event, they should be arranged with the slack increasing away from the critical path. If several paths end at more than one event on the same date, the paths ending at each event should be grouped together and the groups arranged by increasing end-event number.

Paths on which all events are completed may or may not be included in the network. Usually people are concerned more with the work not yet done; so completed paths are omitted. Completed event numbers are marked with the letter "A" and shown at the actual date of completion. Also, if completed paths are left out, the network will get "thinner" in the second dimension as time goes on. The critical path will then always be close to those paths which end in the near future. All activities are shown at their earliest possible completion dates. Slack is indicated at the end of each path between the earliest possible completion date of the last activity and the latest completion date of its ending event. The slack indicator is marked "SSSS" on the activity line. The line representing the activity is a series of digit "1's" printed by the machine.

*The procedure in use.* The procedure has actually been used to print out a detail PERT network. The basic data came from the slack-path sort of the usual Lockheed 7090 PERT output listing. This information was hand-edited to separate completely some slack paths which were not distinguishable by the present Lockheed program. Cards were key-punched for each activity, and extra cards were made for starting each path and indicating the slack position. The paths were studied and arranged in fields for printing according to the rules outlined. It took three days to work out all the details, process all the information, modify a general-purpose 1401 program, and get the results.

The first trial network had a time span of two years and nine months. About 400 activities were involved (most of them in the first year). For the first printing, only 17 fields were printed on a page, and a total of 80 fields were needed. Printing took three minutes for each of the five pages required. The final detail network formed from the five pages was six feet high and fifteen feet long. A section of this network is shown in Exhibit 1.

It was obvious that this printout took up too much space, and the data and program were modified. Fields were reduced from seven to six digits to increase the number of fields from 17 to 20 per page. The time scale was changed from seven to two lines per week (Wednesday and Saturday dates). This resulted in a much more compact

## DETAILED NETWORK PRINTOUT

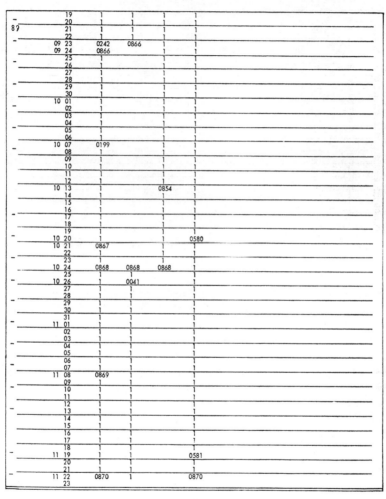

**EXHIBIT 1**

network. Printing time then took one minute per page, or approximately 25 seconds per year. The total size for four pages and two and a half years was four feet by four and a half feet. A section of this network is shown in Exhibit 2.

## COMPACT NETWORK PRINTOUT

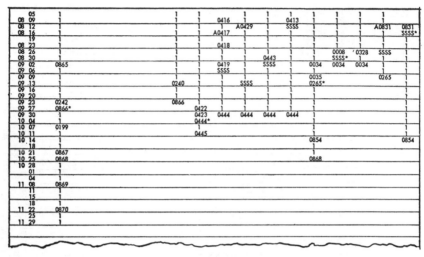

**EXHIBIT 2**

This is still a pioneering effort, and many improvements can and will be made. The project is being studied to consider the value of writing a 7090 or 1401 program which would eliminate the work done so far by hand and punch-card machine procedures. The present 4-digit event-code limitation allows 9999 events to be used in a network, but it would require a conversion listing if the actual event numbers used were five-, six-, or seven-digit capacity allowed by the Lockheed 7090 PERT program.

The present 1401 program is an adaptation of a general-purpose report program. A special program could be more flexible and capable. The present program cannot print activity descriptions or times or the event descriptions. It might be possible to print these separately as labels, which could then be placed on the network at the appropriate locations. The present program prints the horizontal activity line but not the vertical connecting lines. However, a special program could be written to print vertical tie lines; put a letter "V" at the end of each activity line for an arrowhead; change the texture of the path; print the letter "X" for completed paths; print "1" for activities not complete; and print dots instead of "1's" for the slack part of the path.

*The end result.* The output of the present procedure would at least put information in well-organized form for a draftsman to copy in a more artistic type of presentation. This procedure can be used for either a detail or summary PERT network. The only real limitation is the final size of paper a person is willing to accept.

When all the slack is placed at the end of the paths, it implies that work will begin as early as possible and that there is no limit to the resources needed for performing the work. However, it becomes difficult to see at a glance where an activity which is behind schedule is really in a bad situation. The amount of time behind schedule must be compared to the slack at the end of the path.

A different philosophy suggests placing the slack at the beginning of each path, which means starting each activity as late as possible. This gives no protection if any activity should take longer than expected. However, in this case it allows maximum resources to be used on activities which must be completed and tends to prevent a dilution of resources to activities which are not yet urgent.

*Further refinements.* In order to make the printed output look even more like the usual concept of a PERT network, a program should print shapes (such as rectangles) connecting lines and text. There is a 704-705 program used elsewhere in IBM which can satisfy all three requirements.[1] A sample of such a printout is shown in Exhibit 3. One of the FSD groups has worked on the modification of this program with some success.

The basic program was intended to have only a five-by-nine array of rectangles on one page with reference labels indicating connections to other pages. By overlapping page edges, it is possible to extend this concept endlessly. Lines which extend outside the basic page size, however, without a connection at both ends, are presently a problem and would require a modification of the machine program.

Of the many useful features of this program, one of the best is the ease of updating the diagram. If a change has to be made, the change in position of the event block is inserted. The machine then repositions the event block and redraws all the appropriate activity lines in the correct places.

[1] See Case, P. W., H. H. Graff, and M. Kloomak, "The Recording, Checking, and Printing of Logic Diagrams," Proceedings of the Eastern Joint Computer Conference, December 1958.

PRINTOUT NETWORK IN PERT FORM

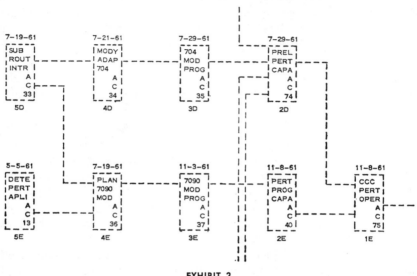

**EXHIBIT 3**

At present the program must be given the position of each of the event blocks. It would be possible to combine the positioning rules of the earlier procedure with this more elegant printing procedure. Because of the size and spacing of the event blocks, it is likely that this type of output would be primarily useful for a summary type of network rather than a detailed one.

Work is going on separately at another research activity in IBM to print out both block shapes and connecting lines without page limitations. This has been shown to be completely possible, starting with a basic PERT program, and it yields the printed network without any human intervention.

Finally, a program has been in existence for some time known as the Flow Charter.[2] This will take a computer program in machine-language instruction form and convert it to a block and line output in flow-chart form.

[2] See Haibt, Lois M., "A Program to Draw Multilevel Flow Charts," Proceedings of the Western Joint Computer Conference, March 1959.

# SECTION IV: ALLIED TECHNIQUES

*No investigation of PERT would be complete without an examination of the techniques which are associated with it, how they differ from PERT, and what their special advantages and applications are. Two of the most important of these allied methods of management planning and control are the critical path method and line of balance.*

# THE CRITICAL PATH METHOD •

## WALTER COSINUKE

---

THE ACCELERATED pace of today's modern technology demands an equally modern advancement in project management and the means of making sound decisions. In the many project activities involving the engineering, construction, and maintenance of today's facilities and installations, the critical path method (CPM) is a powerful management tool that has been used with rewarding results. It integrates all of the factors or building blocks of a project: manpower, money, time, materials, and equipment. It allows management to develop a balanced, optimum, time-cost schedule, which assures timeliness and a minimum use of resources and which provides a true vehicle for management by exception.

PERT contains a feature which CPM lacks—probabilities for the estimates of job duration. However, PERT lacks CPM's cost-time function, which is an important factor in maintaining complete project control. CPM differs from traditional methods of network analysis in two fundamental ways:

1. Planning is separated from scheduling. Planning consists in determining what tasks must be performed to complete a project and what the order of their performance should be. Scheduling is the act of translating the plan into a timetable.

2. Time and costs are directly related. This indicates that the minimum costs and related time of an activity in a project can be shortened at some sacrifice in cost.

---

WALTER COSINUKE is Technical Assistant to the President, Catalytic Construction Company Philadelphia, Pennsylvania.

## THE PLANNING FUNCTION

The critical path technique starts with arrow diagraming, which incorporates all elements of a project. Operations, methods, and resources (time, money, manpower, equipment, and material) plus imposed conditions (design, delivery, approval, budget, completion date, decisions, and so on) are molded into a coordinated plan and model. Each activity, task, or operation is represented as an arrow, and each arrow indicates the existence of a task.

The arrows interconnect to show the sequence in which the tasks will be performed. The result is the diagram, which is, in effect, a network. Three basic questions are asked and answered about each arrow:

1. What must be done before we can start this activity?
2. What can be done concurrently?
3. What must immediately follow this activity?

With a thorough knowledge of the job, only these three questions need be answered to develop a complete network which will serve as a plan for a project.

Arrow diagraming is controlled by the following basic rules, which are necessary for both manual and computer orientation and application:

1. All activities or jobs have an origin and terminal event. The junction of each arrow is called an event. In Exhibit 1, activity *A* has an origin (event 1) and a terminal (event 2). Activity *B* has an origin (event 2) and a terminal (event 3). Event numbers are assigned to the network after the network is completed. A network can be numbered either at random or in sequence order. The controlling factors are whether the calculations will be made manually or by computer and if the latter, what the computer program will allow.

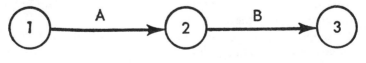

EXHIBIT 1

2. A dummy activity or arrow is used to keep the sequence logically correct. These are shown as dotted-line arrows. They must also have identification and event numbers. Where two or more

activities have common events, dummy arrows are used for all but one of the concerned branches. This is done in order to keep the event numbers separate (see Exhibit 2).

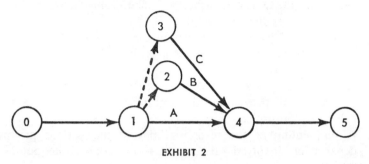

EXHIBIT 2

3. There are many projects where there are sequence relationships. For example, in Exhibit 3, activity *C* will be dependent on the completion of both *A* and *B*. If we inject an activity (*D*) which is dependent on *B* and independent of *A* and *C*, the correct diagram would be as shown: *C* is dependent on *A* and *B*, but *D* depends only on *B* being complete.

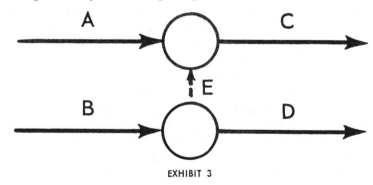

EXHIBIT 3

4. An activity in a network only indicates that the flow is always in one direction from origin (tail) to terminal (head). Its length or direction on paper has no meaning as such.

Although the diagram of a project may consist of hundreds or thousands of arrows, the simple common-sense approach facilitates the task of preparing the diagrammatic model. It forces the people responsible for the project to deal with the problem areas before beginning work. The activities of all groups such as engineering, design, purchasing, and subcontractors are completely delineated. The arrow diagram incorporates all the necessary factors of a project into a logical and sound plan just as it established the relationship between the work elements. It provides the following:

1. A disciplined basis for the planning of a project.
2. A clear picture of the scope of a project that can be easily read and understood.
3. An important vehicle for evaluating strategies and objectives.
4. A means of preventing the omission of jobs that naturally belong to the project.
5. A pinpointing of the responsibilities of the various groups or departments involved—because it shows connections among the jobs.
6. An aid in refining the design of the project.
7. An excellent vehicle for orienting and training project personnel.

## TIME-COST ASSIGNMENT

Once the plan is established and the arrow diagram correctly depicts the logical sequential relationship between project activities, time and cost estimates must be made for all activities in the project to determine project duration, costs, and schedule.

There is a direct relation between the time and cost of any activity. This relationship takes into account the manpower, money, and methods used and the efficiency achieved. There is an optimum way to do a task. When one deviates from this way, sacrifices in cost are made. If a task is dragged out, cost can increase and schedule can be protracted. Let us take as an example a job which requires two men to perform it most efficiently in five days and assume that the nature of this job will not allow any more effort on it. A number of possibilities exist:

1. Two men may work five eight-hour day shifts.
2. Four men may work two shifts and complete—in three days— three day shifts and two night shifts. Shift premiums will make the cost higher than in the first instance.
3. Six men may work three shifts and finish—in two days—two day

shifts, two second shifts, and one third shift. Additional premiums will further increase the cost.

4. If more than six men work, the cost will skyrocket and two days will still be required to do the job.

5. One man will drag out the job for more than ten days and will increase costs because of inefficiencies.

An activity time-cost curve is shown in Exhibit 4. However, CPM does not require us to produce such a curve for each activity in a project (because sufficient data are generally not available); rather, we

## ACTIVITY TIME COST CURVE

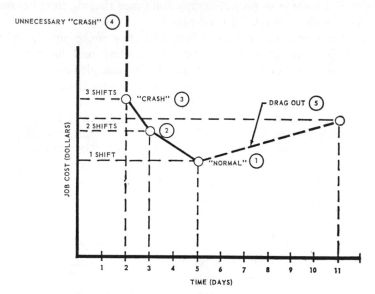

"NORMAL" POINT:   Normal cost is defined as the minimum activity cost, and the related minimum time is defined as normal time.

"CRASH" POINT:   Crash time is defined as the minimum possible time to perform the activity, and the related cost is defined as crash cost.

**EXHIBIT 4**

must estimate the "normal" and "crash" points. A linear relationship between these two points is generally sufficient to produce acceptable results comparable to the accuracy of the data input. Where more accurate information is available, CPM can consider it if needed.

DIRECT PROJECT COST AND SCHEDULE

With this information available for each activity in the project, CPM can be utilized to process the data. Objective information is derived which gives a number of schedules showing the earliest and latest starting and completion times for each activity and their related costs, along with a number of project-completion times ranging from "normal" to "crash" with their related lowest costs.

All critical activities are identified, and they make up the critical path. These activities will have but one starting and finishing time. Delay in any one of them will hold up the completion of the total project. The critical path of a project is the connected sequence of activities that forms the path of longest duration. All the remaining activities in the project can be classified as non-critical. These can suffer a limited amount of time delay in the earliest start and completion time without affecting the project-completion date. The amount of time delay permissible is called "float." Three different types of floats are identified with CPM, and each has a different meaning:

1. Total float is spare time available when all preceding activities start at the earliest possible times and all succeeding activities occur at the latest possible times.
2. Free float is spare time available when all preceding activities start at the earliest possible times and all succeeding activities occur at the earliest possible times.
3. Independent float is spare time available when all preceding activities occur at the latest possible times and all succeeding activities occur at the earliest possible times.

Having ascertained both the activities on the critical path and the amount of float available for the non-critical activities, those managing the project can control them with much greater assurance. They can concentrate their efforts on the critical jobs with complete knowledge of the effect of any changes on the over-all schedule.

Since the duration of any project is dependent on the time required to complete the various activities, it is possible to have a range of durations depending on the selected time needed to perform each activity. This selection of duration also incorporates specific related activity costs. As a result, for each project duration there is a different project cost. In any project a tremendous number of possibilities exist for combining the various activity times and costs. The mathematical algorithms formulated for CPM do this and produce only the lowest possible cost for each project duration. This computation involves a complex mathematical analysis, but the theory can be summarized in terms of the following operations:

1. A normal or minimum cost for project duration is computed.
2. With the minimum cost schedule established, the next step is to seek and compress activities on the critical path that have the smallest change in cost per unit of time saved and consequently cost the least to expedite. A new schedule is then prepared showing the activities that have been compressed to some values between the normal and crash durations.

Compression of these activities along the critical path can result in making other activities critical and producing more critical paths. Further compression must then consider activities along more than the original critical path. The results produce a series of schedules, each establishing the earliest and latest start and completion times as well as floats for all activities on the project. The critical path is identified, and the associated cost for each activity and for the over-all project for each schedule is provided. The cost for each schedule is the minimum for its related project duration.

Let us take as an example the project illustrated in Exhibit 5. The normal duration of this project is nine days with a normal cost of $370. The crash duration is five days with a cost of $520. Let us assume that management wants to develop a seven-day schedule for this project. There are several ways to do this. First of all, only the items on the critical path should be decreased; therefore, job 0-2 will not be changed. Of the three critical items, job 2-3 has the smallest cost increment. Therefore, it should be decreased to one day, which will increase costs by $20. Next, job 0-1 should be decreased since its cost increment is $30 in contrast to $40 for job 1-2. We now have a schedule of seven days' duration with a cost of $370 plus $50, or $420. It should be noted that job 0-2 no longer has float, and all jobs in the project are now critical.

The outlined procedure produces a minimum cost schedule for a

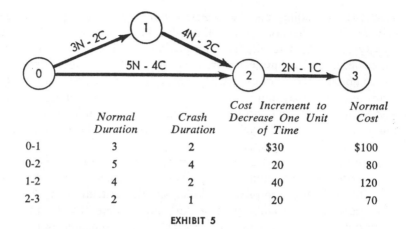

| | Normal Duration | Crash Duration | Cost Increment to Decrease One Unit of Time | Normal Cost |
|---|---|---|---|---|
| 0-1 | 3 | 2 | $30 | $100 |
| 0-2 | 5 | 4 | 20 | 80 |
| 1-2 | 4 | 2 | 40 | 120 |
| 2-3 | 2 | 1 | 20 | 70 |

**EXHIBIT 5**

project ranging from "normal" to "crash." Exhibit 6 is a graphic representation of this point. It also shows other combinations which are more costly in attaining the desired project duration.

TOTAL PROJECT COST CURVES

On commercial projects, cost and return on investment are the primary considerations in setting a project schedule. This optimum point can be determined from a total project cost curve (Exhibit 7) —that is, a summation of the direct project cost curve and the indirect project cost curves. The indirect project cost curves are broken down into two categories.

1. *Market profit losses,* which indicate that if a market is available and the plant can be put into operation sooner, these profit losses will be incurred after the crash duration.
2. *Indirect costs,* which take in the remaining indirect costs and are in many instances the engineering and construction costs. They include overhead, fees, and penalties for not completing on time.

This plotting of cost curves is an excellent tool, but it has a number of disadvantages. First of all, it requires processing on a large computer, which may be costly and difficult to schedule. Second, collecting the input information for each sequence becomes a lengthy, time-consuming chore. All of the input information for the average minimum cost point for each activity is generally available and is based on previous experience and work measurement. The input information for the crash point, however, is difficult to estimate and is a definite trouble spot. Furthermore, after analyzing a number of projects statistically, we have found in our company that approximately 60 per cent of the sequences never deviate from normality in determining the direct cost portion of the project cost curves. Of those that do change, only a minority reach the crash point. The others are decreased somewhere between optimum cost and crash duration.

Realizing the tremendous value of the original tool, Catalytic has evolved a technique called the "step approach." This approach develops only that portion of the project cost curve which is necessary and

## DIRECT PROJECT COST CURVE

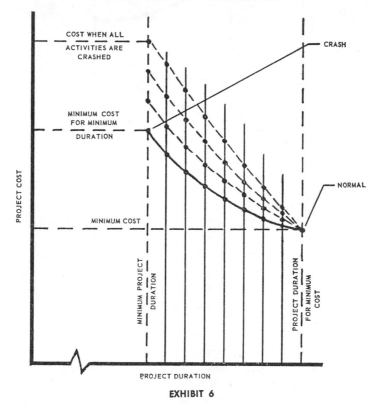

**EXHIBIT 6**

## TOTAL PROJECT COST CURVE

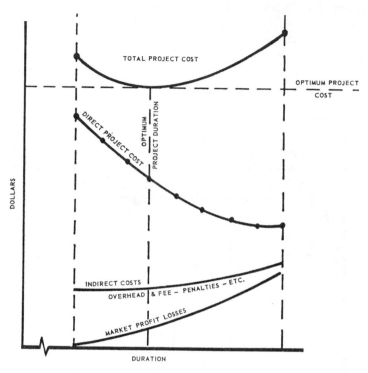

EXHIBIT 7

applicable to the project—that is, from the minimum point of the direct cost to the minimum cost for the over-all project, or optimum duration as shown on the project cost curve.

The first step in this approach is to make an optimum computation on the direct cost portion of the project. Once the minimum cost computation is obtained, the next step is to "squeeze" or shorten the duration of the project. To do this, the activities on the critical path or paths are analyzed, and the ones which will decrease the task one unit of time with the least cost are selected. It is easy to spot these tasks as experience in this approach is gained. New input data for these sequences showing the new durations and their respective incremental increases in cost are inserted into the program, and a new computation is made. The following are ways of "squeezing".

1. Assigning more men to the task.
2. Shifting work or overtime.
3. Paying premiums to vendors for expediting delivery of material and equipment.
4. Seeking other strategies or objectives. For example, when we are faced with the problem of late delivery of a major item on the citical path, the plan can be changed by resequencing the item on the arrow diagram and working around it. The alternate plan would result in some additional cost.
5. Taking risks on preliminary data to get a jump on design in order to gain time. This may result in revising drawings and, at times, work completed in the field. This will add to the cost.

As each computation is made by this "cut and try" method, starting from the minimum direct cost duration, points for the over-all project cost curve should be plotted, using the summation of each of the points on the following curves:

1. Direct cost of labor, equipment, and materials.
2. Indirect cost of administration, overhead, and so forth.
3. Indirect costs such as product or market losses derived from market analysis or economic feasibility studies.

When the over-all project cost curve develops a tendency to increase in cost, the computations can stop because the optimum duration and costs for the over-all project have been determined. This is the point of highest return on the investment and, therefore, optimum project cost. The step approach demands less effort than attempting to estimate crash time and duration for all required activities by the original method; and, if machine computation is used, a much smaller computer is required.

STAGES OF APPLICATION

Application of CPM can be as simple or as complex as a particular program may warrant. At Catalytic, six stages of application have been defined. The stages are of increasing complexity for problems of increasing scope. The steps are as follows:

1. Manual computation to produce a single, normal schedule of earliest start and finish, latest start and finish, total float, free float, and independent float for each activity and to establish an over-all duration for the project.

2. Manual computation to produce a single schedule after compression of activities on the critical path, which establishes earliest start and finish, latest start and finish, total float, free float, and independent float for each activity in a reduced or crash-time project duration.
3. Computer processing of information to produce a spectrum of alternate cost and time schedules.
4. Manual adjustment of floating activities in a given schedule to minimize peak demand for manpower (by craft or specialization) and equipment.
5. Computer processing of floating activities in a given schedule to minimize peak demand for manpower (by craft or specilization) and equipment.
6. Allocation of limited resources, primarily manpower, among several projects; in essence, this is multiproject scheduling.

After the development of the arrow diagram, the step utilizing manual computation to produce the normal schedule is the most widely practiced form of the technique. As experience is gained, the first five steps become working tools for project managers. Multiproject scheduling is used at Catalytic to balance and level manpower, by specialty, and to determine the additional or excessive manpower requirements of the present organization.

*Input data.* At Catalytic the project manager is responsible for developing his own arrow diagram. The first requirement is that the project be broken down into a sufficient number of definable steps to make diagraming practical and worthwhile. Experience has shown that advantages can be gained from arrow diagraming on projects having approximately 20 or more subdivisions. Machine computation is recommended for projects with over 100 activities.

The extent of project breakdown is dependent on the degree of control desired and the over-all scope of the project. (Regardless of the time content of the project and subdivisions, the sequence, method, skill requirements, and objectives must be understood.) On most EPC types of contracts at Catalytic, the arrow diagram is developed in two stages. The preliminary diagram is prepared at the time of bidding or immediately upon award of the contract. The final, refined and expanded diagram follows the completion of the engineering flow sheets and plot plan.

The second requirement concerning input data is that the job break-down and sequence must be clearly defined in writing so that managers, supervisors, and planners are in agreement as to their content. A fine detailed plan is worthless if supervisors have completely different plans for executing the tasks in question.

The third requirement also involves knowledge of job detail. Sufficient understanding of the particular job method, crew size and skills, and timing must be known so that more than one method in terms of time and cost can be visualized for the activities in a project. With this information, a spectrum of schedules relating time to cost can be produced.

*Output data.* The arrow diagram and computation output do not lend themselves to ready or easy use, but from this material a series of subschedules for specific groups is produced. These subschedules can be in the form of machine output or bar charts. In the development of such schedules, a major consideration is leveling and balancing man-power with the total forces available and with the completion date. This can be done either with a manual trial-and-error technique or with a computer-designed program. Since computation output clearly defines what jobs can float in time and to what degree, effective leveling and balancing of manpower against a given schedule can be done in a substantially simpler way with other systems not utilizing CPM.

The first step in the leveling computation is to schedule jobs falling along the critical path and to compute by craft the manpower required to perform these tasks. The next step is to schedule every job at its earliest start date and sum each craft from start to finish time of the project. In most cases, the summation will result in an erratic or "unleveled" manpower schedule. However, by displacing jobs that have float, a leveled craft and total-force curve can be arrived at. If craft manpower needs exceed those available for the project, then a schedule with a longer duration must be adopted. Leveling will establish a stable craft force which will work with higher efficiency and morale and produce tangible savings in costs. In addition, supporting personnel such as supervisors, service crafts, and accounting can be held to a minimum. Tools and equipment required for the project can also be kept at a constant level. The leveling and balancing technique, in short, forces management to make a series of decisions that previously may not have been considered.

Once the subschedules are developed, they should be transmitted to the respective groups concerned. They may then be tied in with over-all methods and work measurement data and similar procedural information so that the plan can be carried out efficiently.

## DETAILED COST CONTROL AND REPORTING

The critical path method, as we have seen, can be used to develop the scope of work, a plan, and a schedule and as a general cost control tool. Two other important features increase the effectiveness of this technique—detailed cost control and reporting.

It is important to note that CPM starts with the conception of a project where detailed information on design is not known. As definitive details become available, engineering, purchasing, and job orders are prepared to establish a more detailed plan, a more efficient means of work measurement, and a system of controls. These orders become the cost control centers, and the critical path network becomes the master cost control tool. On small projects, control can be applied to each activity. But on larger projects, this approach would create too many cost control centers and thereby increase the probability of error in the feedback and reporting data.

The unit of work selected for each order must be directly related to the critical path diagram. The order may be made up of a number of activities on the network, or one activity can be broken down into a number of orders. The unit of work should be as large as possible to avoid the cumbersome detail in reporting and control that would result from many small orders. On the other hand, it should be small enough to permit control in reporting and administering the job. Moreover, it should be set up in such a manner that the unit costs derived from each order can be used to evaluate future work which is of a similar nature.

With the engineering, purchasing, or job order complete, suitable methods must be employed to translate the analysis into the practical work guide which will coordinate the efforts of the project force. A daily work schedule is used for this purpose. This schedule together with the orders, critical path network, and over-all schedule will answer the basic questions of the engineering and construction forces and its service groups: where, when, and how all items of project work will be done on the following day.

Time and materials costs are reported and accumulated against the orders for processing and posting of the cost control report, which is designed to act as a signaling system to those responsible and should be issued frequently enough to insure dynamic control over costs. It is a means of reporting the status of each order on a periodic basis. The comparisons of per cent complete to per cent expended and estimated man-hours to indicated final man-hours pinpoint areas or activities which are exceeding costs. This information is made available in time to permit supervisors to adjust the work accordingly so that

## CPM PROJECT CONTROL CURVE

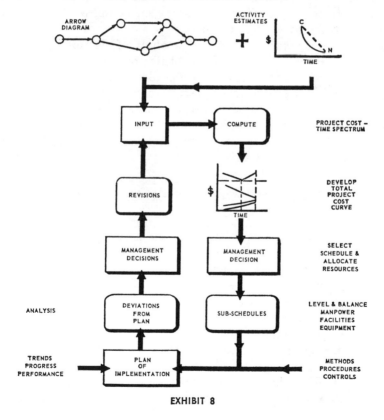

EXHIBIT 8

budget costs can be met. Trends can be established early for unit costs of a certain type of activity, and indicated final estimates can be made from these trends. The computing and predicting of trends is a task that requires elemental time values, experience, and a certain amount of research.

The reporting of progress is the final link in an effective project control system. Measurement of work completed as compared to the total project effort has always been a major problem in cost control programs. However, with a detailed order system where standard time data are utilized for work measurement, this problem is somewhat simplified. Each order can be weighed as a percentage of the total job; and, when it is completed, that portion of the total job is completed. When measuring the work accomplished on an uncompleted order, that portion of the sequence that has been completed is of course compared to the total effort required.

If we have a complete plan and analysis of the total job, along with a measurement of trends and completion of orders, it then becomes a relatively simple task to develop a reporting system. There are many ways in which this can be accomplished, such as the Gantt charts and data-processing tabulation. One very effective way is to utilize the network of the critical path and, with colored marking tapes, indicate the status of each activity on the project. The CPM project control cycle is shown in Exhibit 8.

## COROLLARY ADVANTAGES OF CRITICAL PATH

The critical path technique has many corollary advantages:
1. It provides the project manager with specific information that permits him to set an objective and rigorous schedule and to discuss with his management or client, on a practical basis, why that schedule was chosen and what considerations will be involved in changing it.
2. With dynamic reporting and updating, the technique provides top management with an integrated summary picture of total progress and progress outlook on a continuous basis.
3. It simplifies the communications problem through a detailed action plan using a common language for all groups. The prepa-

ration of the plan requires job responsibilities to be clearly pin-pointed. Failure to meet schedule times can be checked periodically against the original plan, and the true cause for failing to meet completion dates can be clearly stated.

4. CPM tightens up work performance and reveals inadequacies in methods, individual skills, supervisory direction, and manpower balance. Many times, improvements in control practices and supervision are necessary.

5. It places a dollar value on change. Thus able to relate time schedules to cost, management can readily justify methods improvement. Most important, methods work can be directed to those portions of a project or shutdown where the greatest gain for the least expenditure of dollars and technical effort can be achieved.

# LINE OF BALANCE •

## *I. Its Value in Manufacturing Operations*

**REAR ADMIRAL GEORGE T. MUNDORFF, U.S.N. (RET.)**

---

THE DIRECTION AND CONTROL of major weapons systems programs at General Precision is vested in a program manager, who is fully responsible for establishing and exercising technical and administrative control over the entire program. He has been given the necessary authority to discharge his assigned responsibilities and has been provided with all the management tools that are needed for the satisfactory performance of his function.

Our Management Control System is designed to achieve the efficient and economical utilization of resources. Properly installed and implemented, it enables management to concentrate its full attention on the direction of the program, and it obviates unnecessary diversion of effort. Its thesis is this: The proper combination of those controls which are internal to the program and those which are an inalienable function of top executives, both facilitated by the rapid exchange of accurate information, is a fundamental ingredient of effective program management.

The basic principles of this management system are equally applicable to simple projects which lie wholly within the province of a single individual and to the most comprehensive type of program which requires facilities and specialized talents which can be mustered only in a multidivisional effort. Regardless of the amount of effort involved, we tailor our system to suit each individual program. In this way, the structure is never made more complex than the situation demands. When

---

REAR ADMIRAL GEORGE T. MUNDORFF, U.S.N. (RET.) is Staff Assistant, Librascope Division, General Precision Inc., Burbank, California.

necessary, the program manager has available for his assistance the full range of data-processing and computer technology. Depending upon the nature of the program under consideration, the controls to be exercised may include pertinent extractions from line of balance, PERT, critical path, and such variations of them as the milestone and day-control reporting systems.

LINE OF BALANCE

Line of balance may be defined as "an effective technique for measuring, collecting, interpreting, and presenting facts—time, cost, and accomplishment—all measured against a specific plan." It is founded on the principles of good management: (1) there must be a stated objective—a target which we have identified as our common goal; (2) there must be a clearly defined plan for reaching that objective; (3) there must be some way of knowing current status— that is, a measurement of the progress being made; and (4) there must be a means of comparing actual accomplishment with planned progress. These elements will tend to provide for the continuous exercise of authority and create a balanced, coordinated, single operation out of a large number of individual transactions.

Line of balance satisfies the following requirements of good management: (1) it serves as a tool for reaching timely decisions; (2) it clearly identifies any element not proceeding according to plan; (3) it not only shows what has been done but also forecasts future accomplishment; (4) it fosters orderly thinking and develops disciplined performance; and (5) it provides a means of communication, both vertical and lateral, progressively condensed as the organizational level increases.

Any operation can be analyzed through a simple but orderly process of reduction. After this analysis has been done and the results stated in chart form, the controlling factors can be quickly and easily identified at any time by scanning the four characteristic elements found in the line of balance charts. These charts make it possible to communicate the status and the objective of any program to all levels of the organization.

The line of balance technique operates on the principle of *exception* —that is, it concentrates attention on deviations from planned performance and not on a continuous examination of the plan as a whole. We start with a mass of detail at the base of an operation and reduce it by successive synthesis to three reporting levels. Some one of these will satisfy the reporting needs of any level of management.

However, it should be emphasized that successful functioning of the system is entirely dependent upon a sound foundation, accurate reporting, and a solid understanding of what is required and when. This is also true of any other management system. Failure to make a decision is often tantamount to *making* a decision. This is because a decision by default is just as binding as (and often more costly than) determining a course of action on the basis of careful, analytical judgment.

Among the advantages of line of balance are the following:

1. It is flexible. The system is modified to suit the installation; it does not require the alteration of any procedure that is functioning satisfactorily.
2. It is effective from the earliest stage of development until completion of production. There is no need to change the system, whether the process is a repetitive or a one-time effort.
3. It provides a clear channel of communication throughout the establishment. A suitable display is available for every level of organization and is never more detailed than is actually required.
4. It provides cost and manpower controls, including a firm understanding of the amount of contingency included in an established budget. It identifies critical assets and tells when and where they are required.
5. It fixes responsibilities and establishes the ground rules for common understanding. It defines the scope of the job and designates the person or persons responsible for its accomplishment.
6. It anticipates the future and gives timely warning of impending deviations from the plan. It serves to identify the points where decisions and actions are required.

ONE COMPANY'S ACCOMPLISHMENTS WITH LINE OF BALANCE

Let us examine one instance in which the line of balance technique led to major benefits. A firm which we will call the Federal Manufacturing Company was experiencing serious difficulty in turning out the items which it had contracted to produce: it had failed to meet an

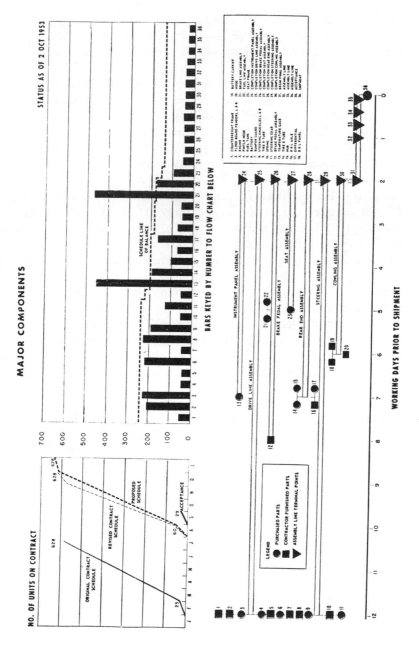

original schedule. After a reorganization of the company and the creation of a new schedule, production appeared to be no better. Obviously, a detailed review was in order, and a series of line of balance charts was prepared.

In the exhibit on page 167 we see the original, revised, and proposed schedules and the actual deliveries made to date. The plan of operation shows how each major component fits into the assembly process and the point in the cycle where it is required to be available. Each of these points is marked by a symbol that is keyed by a corresponding number to a bar graph which indicates the number of end-item sets that had been used or were available for use at the time of the survey. For example, we can see that No. 13 represents the receipt of temperature gauges (a major element of the instrument-panel assembly) at a point which is seven days prior to shipment of the finished tractor. Reference to the chart discloses that approximately 450 sets of these gauges were used or were available for use. The chart also shows that at the same time no more than 200 of these sets were required for the satisfaction of current production requirements. This is indicated by the dotted line, which is the line of balance. Comparison of the height of each bar in the graph with the level indicated by the line of balance provides an instantaneous measure of program status and required accomplishment. Basically, the picture is that of a fairly difficult situation in which most of the items are below the line of balance.

Another chart was developed to show the status of all purchased parts and it was evident that parts procurement was not in balance with program requirements: parts which were required early in the production cycle were in short supply. Inventories of other items were unnecessarily large. This suggested that there was a weak or ineffective purchasing plan. In a similar chart of the company-furnished parts situation, the bar graph depicted the worst situation in each family group. At a glance it was seen that production control was attempting to maintain a uniform level of output for all parts. The line of balance showed that correct production levels varied from item to item, depending upon when they were required. Further examination revealed that the stock level of one of the earliest-required parts was no more than about 42 end-item sets. This literally meant that production was limited to 42 tow tractors, no matter how many other parts were on hand. Similar comments could have been made about the remaining items, since all were below the line of balance.

The next step was to summarize the data presented in these three charts. In each instance the worst item in each category was taken and plotted as a summary of the whole. The composite picture then showed the situation to be in serious difficulty. Therefore, management decided to do something about it. It established an organized plan for Purchasing to follow and also fixed priorities for expediting parts. Production Control was required to re-examine its manufacturing schedule in order to provide adequate quantities of parts at appropriate times.

Two months later the charts showed that the company had achieved a production rate approximately equal to that required, although the total quantity was considerably below the level which should have been attained. Nevertheless, a marked improvement was taking place in all areas. Finally, three weeks in advance of the proposed delivery schedule, all deliveries were satisfactorily completed primarily as a result of the line of balance technique.

THE BASIC TECHNIQUE EXPLAINED

The mechanics by which a line of balance is constructed and the fundamental theory underlying this technique are relatively simple. In the exhibit on page 167, we see in the upper left-hand portion that the proposed schedule calls for the delivery of 200 units by October 2. In the plan of operation (the lower half of the exhibit), we also see that the point of shipment, indicated at the extreme right, corresponds to these 200 units. It is quite obvious, however, that there must be a number of additional units at each of the various stages throughout the manufacturing cycle. The number of incomplete units, and their required state of completion if the delivery schedule is to be met, may be readily determined by a logical procedure.

Consider the items designated by numbers 1 through 11. The plan of operation indicates that they are required 12 days in advance of the shipping date. Clearly, then, in this particular instance we must have used or have available for use not only the 200 end-item sets required for delivery on October 2 but an additional quantity sufficient to meet the shipping needs 12 working days afterward. We can determine that the quantity corresponding to a shipping date 12 working days later is

240 units by drawing a vertical line from the base line at a point corresponding to October 17, the date in question. We project the intersection of this vertical line and the proposed-schedule curve in a horizontal direction in order to establish the required levels for items 1 through 11.

Another example is the requirement for brake-pedal assembly, item 12, which is established in the same way. We see that the assembly plan calls for its incorporation at a point 8 days prior to shipment, we draw a vertical line at October 11, and we find that 200 units should have been used or been available for use. By following the same principles of construction, requirement levels for all other elements are drawn. This results in the familiar step-down curve of the line of balance. This comparison between actual inventories and the line of balance affords a graphic portrayal of program status and a ready forecast of shipping capability.

FURTHER APPLICATIONS FOR LINE OF BALANCE

This case study affords us an illustration of the benefits which accrue to those managers who take time to work out a thorough plan for their operation. It involved the process of fabrication and assembly. Line of balance can be applied to other manufacturing or production operations—whether job shop or flow shop. However, during the 20 years that have passed since the introduction of this technique, it has been applied across the entire spectrum of program types. All of these installations have one thing in common: the outputs and conclusions are dependent upon the validity of the experience data and the quality of the analytical processes from which they are derived. Mechanization will speed up the operation, but it cannot make any other contribution, nor will it substitute for human judgment or bolster an inadequate decision.

Among the other areas in which line of balance has worked out extremely well are system development programs. Line of balance control was used in the Federal Aviation Agency's development of a semiautomated air-traffic-control system for the national airways. Since equipment development is a part of system development, it follows that this is another area in which line of balance also will prove to be beneficial. Even in the area of pure research it will be found helpful. The discipline imposed by a need to plan, the psychological impact of having established an orderly program of events, and the existence of formal budgets all tend to insure the more efficient expenditure of time and money. One of the most amazing and profitable applications of line of balance is in the field of engineering test. One company, by simply rearranging the test program in an orderly manner and by improving the communications link between checkout and engineering, was able to effect a saving in excess of 30 per cent. Similar savings in time and effort have been realized in other organizations.

# II. Application to Engineering

**WILLIAM BLOOM**

---

A T GENERAL PRECISION emphasis is placed on advanced management control techniques to monitor the progress of programs and to enable management to make timely and accurate decisions. The best features of each of the new and improved techniques—such as PERT, critical path, milestone reporting, and line of balance—are used to form a completely integrated tool for the use of management. Initially, the line of balance technique was used to monitor major production jobs. When it was recognized that it was applicable to other activities—especially engineering—it was further refined and developed to broaden its field of application.

Four major factors are common to both engineering and manufacturing: performance, budget, internal inputs, and external inputs. Data on performance, especially delivery, are essential in both activities

---

WILLIAM BLOOM is Manager, Management Controls, General Precision Inc., Tarrytown, New York.

whether we are dealing with study programs, prototypes, or production units. Budgets and actual costs also play an important part because profit or loss is dependent on the extent to which they are controlled. In addition, internal coordination and cooperation are equally vital. Moreover, whether we are dealing with customer engineering data or vendor parts for manufacturing, it is imperative that we have reliable external inputs to assure effective management controls.

Let us examine the steps involved in management control. The first is to determine the project concept. Once this is done, we set forth the subsystem and component specifications. This is followed by detailed design work, the construction and testing of a breadboard model, the building of the prototype, and, finally, the manufacture of production units.

These steps are managed by developing a basic plan, listing specific tasks, which breaks down the job into major and minor subdivisions and then further subdivides it into the smallest element that is reasonable to consider. The relationship of each task to the broad program objectives is also spelled out in detail. When the basic elements which govern the project have been determined, the construction of the detailed plans can proceed.

Estimates of man-hours and material costs for these tasks which follow are based upon past experience and extrapolated for untried tasks. The next step is the sequencing of the tasks, which is undertaken with a full realization of the risks involved in paralleling the operations. This information must then be appraised in the light of available manpower and material, and other work in progress or planned must be taken into consideration. It is in the preparation of this detailed plan that many people see for the first time the specific interrelationships of the elements, the timing that is required, and the critical areas that control subsequent action.

A MANAGEMENT CONTROL SYSTEM

The planning principles have been translated at General Precision into a set of controls which extend from initial analysis at the proposal level to the preparation and updating of management control charts. These controls can be classified into two groups: internal and external.

*Internal controls.* Our internal controls include an integrated set of procedures for establishing and monitoring performance and cost operations within a project. These techniques include a clear statement of project organization, personnel, and responsibilities; establishment of uniformly applied ground rules; provision for task analysis and input-output analysis; man-loading and critical facilities; a design-order numbering system; work-order authorizations; individual flow diagrams; and cost and performance feedback.

*External controls.* Internal controls permit the preparation and maintenance of highly reliable PERT networks or level-III line of balance charts, and they are specifically designed for levels of supervision directly responsible for getting the work done. However, the higher echelons of management need information of a more distilled nature. To provide this, my company has encouraged the development and use of techniques for controls which are external to the project. These include: (1) PERT summary charts or level-II line of balance charts and (2) level-I line of balance charts and deviation reports with supporting detailed information.

In addition, management relies upon personnel who are trained in the principles and use of management controls. Management is also aided by briefings, memos, and visual displays for the dynamic reporting of status and the regular examination of program status in order to direct top management's attention to existing and anticipated problem areas. Once data collection and processing are mechanized, there will be more rapid analysis and dissemination of management status reports.

ITS USE IN ENGINEERING

A typical example of the application of line of balance to an engineering prototype involved a flight simulator which was under development by General Precision's Link Division. Included among the control charts for the program was a level-III integrated flow diagram and a supervisor's schedule or individual flow diagram. The first step was the preparation of a provisional level-II chart, which represented the tentative plan for the design and fabrication of the simulator and which was adjusted on the basis of the information that was generated by the supporting charts.

The next step was to build a schedule and budget for each of the

## LEVEL-II LINE OF BALANCE CHART

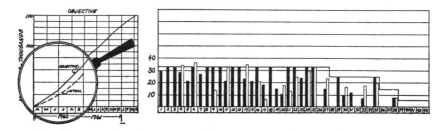

supervisors, which set forth in detail their specific goals and the types of information required by scheduled dates. This information was then integrated into the flow diagram, which summarized the material at the project manager's level and made it possible to identify readily the problems and actions required to maintain the project schedule at the proper level.

Once the detailed plan was available, key points were selected for the level-II line of balance chart (see exhibit). This chart sets forth the activities and decisions from the time of contract award to the delivery of the end item. To the left of the chart is the program schedule, which gives an over-all picture of the budgeted and actual expenditures, expressed in terms of time. Actual progress of the plan is represented by two vertical bars which correspond to each sensor point. A solid bar indicates progress, while a hollow bar reflects the current status of expenditures. Actual and planned progress and expenditures at each sensor point are compared and related on a percentage basis to the line of balance level. This level represents expenditures and accomplishments required to maintain the program schedule.

By comparing the bars that reflect program progress with the line of balance, top management was able to identify quickly the current and anticipated problem areas. For example, one sensor was delinquent because the task was approximately 75-per-cent complete while expenditures had reached almost 90 per cent of budget. The problem was that the information required from the customer was still missing and this was delaying the system designer's efforts. Expenditures exceeded the scheduled budget because several false starts were made as a result of inadequate data. Further action required, according to the report, was for management to inform the customer that unless the necessary data were forthcoming by a specific date, there would be a delay in the delivery of the end item.

The ease with which the line of balance technique promotes effective communications for the various levels of management was evidenced when a level-II sensor was traced through the details in the lower level of charts. This could be done readily because the data were condensed and synthesized—but not altered—as they were processed for successive management review and action. Additional details on the system design were presented in the integrated flow diagram where facts were further amplified by the more detailed charts used by the supervisors. Among the tasks that were delinquent because of inadequate customer data were scale change, cone of ambiguity, and channel select. Thus it was impossible for top management to review the over-all status of the project and (if necessary) to identify in any degree of detail the current problem areas requiring its attention.

### OPERATION AT THE CORPORATE LEVEL

Let us now examine the operation of the system at the corporate level within another division of our company. First, the planning cycle is initiated at the proposal-preparation stage. Once top management has decided to bid, management control techniques are used to gather the information and to present the data. Using the guidelines set forth in the tentative line of balance charts, the supervisors prepare their individual flow diagrams. This information is then combined into an integrated flow diagram, which contains the necessary schedule and budget adjustments. A level-II line of balance chart and accompanying comments on anticipated critical areas are submitted in order to provide assurance of performance capability.

If the proposal is successful, the plan is quickly reviewed and updated. The program manager issues work authorizations which are based upon detailed planning; then the operating personnel start to work. Monitoring of performance and cost is accomplished by both the individual and the integrated flow diagrams. However, this information is too detailed for higher levels of management and therefore must be distilled into a more condensed and usable form. The level-II and level-I line of balance formats give a concise presentation of essential data and allow timely decision making.

The level-I chart gives top management concise data that reflect program status, free of unessential details. It must also provide ready identification of the current or anticipated problem areas. Level-II charts, which are monitored by the senior echelons of divisional management, provide the essential facts and the basis for quick decisions at the subsystem level. At the third level are the flow diagrams, which provide the necessary detail for any level of supervision that is directly responsible for the work.

APPLICATION TO A MAJOR DEVELOPMENT PROGRAM

The Federal Aviation Agency's Management Control Program for its Data Processing Central System offers an excellent example of the application of line of balance to a major development program. Although the data have been modified for simplicity and clarity, they indicate the major tasks of coordinating large numbers of personnel and equipment to meet specific objectives. However, what follows is limited to the test and evaluation of a semiautomatic system of air traffic control.

The testing and evaluation programs were organized into three groups: Group I—enroute; Group III—transition and terminal; and Group II—SAPO, an abbreviated system-test capability. In view of the urgency of the program, testing and evaluation activities were to be carried on in parallel where possible. The test and evaluation operations of the three groups were presented in a provisional level-I chart, which gives a cursory indication of the major activities and their tentative time schedules.

Next came the establishment of ground rules and assumptions to be used in the preparation of the line of balance charts. Some were standard, while others were tailored to fit the situation. The following are examples of these rules and assumptions: (1) delivery of equipment to be made to the test center in accordance with the latest approved delivery schedule; (2) spare parts to be furnished by FAA, with peculiar spares supplied by the contractor; and (3) FAA to provide, install, and maintain government-furnished equipment.

On the basis of these rules, the detailed tasks were broken down into the following categories: (1) equipment installation, test, interconnection test, specification, maintenance, and programing; (2) subsystem and system function tests and test specifications; and (3) planning and control of the operation. This was followed by the measurement of tasks in terms of man-hours and material. For the detailed task breakdown, the supervisors used actual experience on comparable equipment wherever possible and careful judgment in the projection of past experience into unknown areas.

The information was then translated into an individual flow diagram, which illustrated one of the tasks—the installation, installation testing, and interconnecting testing of Peripheral Sector Console (PSC). A sensor indicated that PSC would be delivered by March 1960. The completion of this task was to be the release of the interconnection test specifications by August of that year, but because of delivery delays PSC did not reach the test site until June. Therefore, the supervisor noted the changes on the flow diagram, including the new estimated completion date of November 5, 1960.

The individual flow diagrams were combined into ten integrated flow charts to test the feasibility of the individual plans and to provide a basis for the orderly review of the detailed operations. The input-output and the manpower and critical-facilities charts were examined to determine possible conflicts which would make the plan impracticable. It was discovered that an adjustment had to be made in computer time. This problem was solved by a longer workweek, by eliminating all but essential work, and by adjusting some of the individual flow diagrams.

The Group-I integrated flow diagram consisted of 350 sensors that were broken into five categories: buffer equipment, "R"-register equipment, data processing, functional tests, and miscellaneous. The displayed information was condensed into a level-II line of balance chart. There were four other level-II charts to cover other aspects.

Then the five level-II charts were merged into an over-all level-I summary chart for top management. This chart presented a consolidation of the installation of the three groups of equipment, the functional and operational testing, and the over-all administration. As in the case of the level-II chart sensors (which represented a group of events on lower-level charts) each of the level-I sensors reflected a group of sensors on the level-II chart. The estimated cumulative man-hours and material expenditures of the plan were also indicated. The objective curve for the level-I chart represented the estimated cumulative dollar expenditures for the entire program rather than the man-hours, which reflected the primary expenditure of the level-II chart.

After the installation of the system, a feedback of information was needed to close the loop and measure results. The deviation report and the financial status sheet provided the basis for updating the program. Starting with the integrated flow diagram for Group I, each of the sensors was filled in upon completion; this progress was recorded in a chart which covered the program status as of September 30, 1960. The sensors that were behind schedule were immediately evident.

Thus, the line of balance program provided FAA with a clear, concise picture of each level of activity based upon a well-integrated plan which presented the program objectives. By using the system, management was able to identify problem areas quickly and make timely decisions.

APPLICATION TO OTHER AREAS

In addition to its use in the fields of manufacturing and engineering, the line of balance technique has been applied to other areas such as planning, budgeting, and logistics. For example, a detailed analysis of the impact of alternative appropriations on the readiness requirements of a military facility was used to guide top-level decisions.

The role of line of balance, in brief, is as follows: For top management it is an effective reporting and decision-making device; for middle management it is a method for quickly revealing the status of the program and required action; and for line supervisors it is a technique for identifying and monitoring performance and cost.

# AN EVALUATION OF PERT •

GABRIEL N. STILIAN

---

$M$ANAGERIAL EVALUATION of an operating program is admittedly one of the most important yet most difficult tasks that an executive faces. Many approach this task by using an unsystematic method which determines only whether a particular program should be continued or abandoned. PERT as a management information and decision-making system should be evaluated just like any other initial investment or continuous operating expenditure in a company.

After all, corporate officers must look at the total company operation and evaluate all programs with the board of directors and stockholders in mind. In fact, the function of top management is to allocate the money that is available to it (from the initial investment of the owners and the income derived from sales) to (1) those functions that are necessary for the continuance and growth of sales, (2) the protection and generation of profit margins, and (3) the reduction of costs in order to optimize the profits for the company as a whole not only on a short-range basis but also from a long-range point of view. Profit protection and growth are essential to the health and stability of a company in today's competitive environment.

Each department within a company should concentrate on total objectives as they affect stockholders, employees, and the general public. The PERT system has often been introduced into a firm without relating it to these objectives—that is, without comparing the cost of PERT with the benefits derived from it. Unless PERT proves its value, there is no justification whatsoever for adding it to the many other activities of an organization. Management cannot accept the fact that PERT will produce a profit on blind faith. It must develop precise measures for appraising PERT's profit contribution and, in fact, that of all systems that utilize expensive computer time. Indeed, those companies that have had the most serious problems and the least success with such systems are the ones with no provision for periodic evaluation.

It is entirely reasonable, therefore, to apply the traditional concept of return on investment or some similar yardstick to the PERT system to see that the cost of installing and operating it are in proportion to the expected profit. There is no reason why measures cannot be developed on a quantitative basis, although it is true that only very rough approximations may be possible. Nevertheless, one of the essentials of proper evaluation is *quantitative* as well as *qualitative* appraisal.

A serious inadequacy that too often is encountered in business management today is the tendency to introduce "profitless changes." Many companies have been making changes at a reckless rate of speed and on a basis that is far from sound. These profitless changes have been cutting into today's continuously narrowing profit margins. Top management has failed to exercise the strict control that is required to stop this trend.

Experience has already shown that PERT, the critical path method, line of balance, and all the other network analysis techniques are just as likely to fall into the category of profitless changes as any other business activity. Therefore, evaluation is important not only to justify the installation of the system but also to insure the selection of the particular technique or combination of techniques best suited to the problems and situation of a particular company.

Too many companies have looked upon PERT as a technique that can be picked up in its entirety and installed without adapting it to the organization's needs. This is obviously not the right approach; none of the network analysis techniques can be considered to be universally applicable. The character of one company is never exactly the same as that of another. Each is made up of many different personalities. Management has to recognize this fact in the installation and operation of PERT. Furthermore, the PERT system must be modified, if necessary, in order to be integrated with other management information systems already existing within the company. It is more important to make PERT a practical and meaningful management tool than to preserve it as a separate technique reserved for the specialists.

Although many PERT systems have been justified and installed for contractual reasons, this approach can result in only temporary effectiveness. Regardless of how essential PERT is for contract fulfillment, it is most valuable only when it is used for decision making by the company's line executives. We must remember that PERT's role is not analogous to that of many control systems which provide historical data for evaluation after the fact. Instead, it is a system that provides information for decision making beforehand at the point of action.

To make this system permanently valuable to the operation managers who produce the profits on which the organization's well-being depends, the thinking behind PERT must go far beyond the concept of meeting contractual obligations. If these obligations are the only reason for installing a PERT system, it is very likely that there will be no real contribution to profits. This profitability approach by no means underestimates the value of those PERT schedules which shorten the time needed to complete an urgent project. In fact, the time factor is equally valid when PERT is seen as primarily a profitable decision-making tool.

The significant aspect of a network analysis system is the planning and control that it makes possible—not the methods used in collecting and processing information. In other words, how that information may be generated is unimportant; a computer-based system is no more meaningful in terms of ultimate value to the company than one which uses punched-card equipment, traditional office machines, or clerical effort.

In many instances, those individuals who are responsible for decision making are able to see what is going to happen visually—by reviewing PERT information—even before the reports that identify problem areas are formally written up and issued. This is the strength of PERT. The many elements of the PERT system—the planning sessions, the reporting system, the evaluation sessions—point the way to sound decision making. These, then, are the aspects of PERT that should be emphasized so that the system will not be thrown out of focus by excessive concentration on the details of data collection and processing—to the neglect of flexibility and timeliness. The computer and the punched cards are important only because, as the project becomes larger, more complex hardware is required to process the information fast enough.

It is entirely possible that management may eventually accept a PERT-like approach for the development of a universal management information system—one that will give the individual executive a formalized, meaningful approach to the integrated and precise management of those functions for which he is responsible. The PERT system can be used, so to speak, to design a production line or a production process for the "manufacturer" of a market research study, in marketing; a design for a new product, in R&D; a conversion project or an equipment installation, in manufacturing; a computer installation, in finance; an office move, in the administrative area; a manpower analysis, in personnel; or any number of other "managerial products." The only danger is that we may become so involved in the mechanics of PERT that we will overlook its great promise for the planning and control of a manager's work.

# BIBLIOGRAPHY

ARTICLES


Astrachan, A., "Better Plans Come From the Study of Anatomy of an Engineering Job," *Business Week*, March 21, 1959.

Borklund, William, "Why Polaris Is Winning Its Race Against Time," *Armed Forces Management*, December 1958.

Boulanger, David G., "Program Evaluation and Review Technique," *Advanced Management*, July-August 1961.

Christian, Roger W., "Production Gets . . . A Crystal Ball That Works," *Factory*, July 1961.

Conlin, Paul, "How Goes Military Mobility?" *Armed Forces Management*, June 1961.

Fazar, Willard, "Program Evaluation and Review Technique," *Statistical Reporter*, January 1959.

———, "Progress Reporting in the Special Projects Office," *Navy Management Review*, April 1959.

Ford, L. R., and Fulkerson, D. R., "A Simple Algorithm for Finding Maximal Network Flows and an Application to the Hitchcock Problem," *Canadian Journal of Mathematics*, 1957.

Francis, Harold G., and Pearlman, Jerome, "PERT—Program Evaluation and Review Techniques," *Functional Information Bulletin* (Operations Research and Synthesis Consulting Service, General Electric Company), October 1960.

Freeman, Raoul J., "An Appraisal of Scientific Techniques in R&D Management," *Proceedings of the IRE Winter Convention on Military Electronics*, February 1962.

———, "A Generalized PERT," *Operations Research*, March-April 1960.

———, "Quantitative Methods in Research Management," *California Management Review*, Summer 1960.

Frishberg, M. C., "LESS Tells You How Project Is Doing," *Hydrocarbon Processing & Petroleum Refiner*, February 1962.

Fulkerson, D. R., "A Network Flow Computation for Project Cost Curves," *Management Science*, January 1961.

Gehringer, A. C., "Line of Balance," *The Armed Forces Comptroller*, June 1961.

Hamlin, Fred, "How PERT Predicts for the Navy," *Armed Forces Management*, July 1959.

Healy, Thomas L., "Activity Subdivision and PERT Probability Statements," *Operations Research*, May-June 1961.

Hollis, Cecil R., "Programming for Control of Contract Performance," *NAA Bulletin*, March 1960.

Hull, Seabrook, "The Polaris Program," *Missile Design and Development,* January 1961.

"Industry Borrows POLARIS Planning," *Product Engineering,* June 16, 1958.

Kelley, James E., Jr., "Critical-Path Planning and Scheduling: Mathematical Basis," *Operations Research,* May-June 1961.

Klass, Philip J., "PERT/PEP Management Tool Use Grows," *Aviation Week,* November 28, 1960.

Leavitt, Harold, and Whisler, T. L., "Management in the 1980's," *Harvard Business Review,* November-December 1958.

Lewis, James, "Where PERT Is Headed," *Armed Forces Management,* July 1961.

Malcolm, D. G., "Extensions and Application of PERT as a System Management Tool," *Proceedings of 7th National Conference of The Armed Forces Management Association,* Washington, D. C., February 1961.

Malcolm, D. G., Roseboom, J. H., Clark, C. E., and W. Fazar, "Application of a Technique for Research and Development Program Evaluation," *Operations Research,* September-October 1959.

" 'MAPS' for Managers Show Problem Areas of Big Defense Jobs," *The Wall Street Journal,* August 16, 1961.

Martino, R. L., "How 'Critical-Path' Scheduling Works," *Canadian Chemical Processing,* February 1960.

————, "New Way to Analyze and Plan Operations and Projects Will Save You Time and Cash," *Oil/Gas World,* September 1959.

Mundorff, George T., and Bloom, William, "Industrial Programming Needs Improving," *Armed Forces Management,* January 1958.

"The Navy's Future in Space," *Navy,* April 1961.

"Navy's PERT Way of Building Polaris Gives Industry a Potent New Management Weapon," *Purchasing Week,* April 17, 1961.

"New Tools for Job Management," *Engineering News Record,* January 28, 1961.

Niemann, Ralph A., and Learn, Robert N., "Mechanization of PERT System Provides SP Timely Information," *Navy Management Review,* August 1960.

Pearlman, Jerome, "Engineering Program Planning and Control Through the Use of PERT," *IRE Transactions on Engineering Management,* December 1960.

"PERT," *Data Processing Digest,* May 1961.

"Power for Peace," *Time,* August 1, 1960.

"Progress Reporting in the Special Progress Office for the Fleet Ballistic Missile Program," *Navy Management Review,* April 1959.

Sayer, J. S., Kelley, J. E., Jr., and Morgan R. Walker, "Presentation on PERT System," *Factory,* July 1960.

Schriever, Lt. Gen. Bernard A., "We Had Youth," *Armed Forces Management,* February 1961.

Villers, Raymond, "The Scheduling of Engineering Research," *The Journal of Industrial Engineering,* November-December 1959.

PAMPHLETS

Archibald, Russell D., *PEP as a Management Tool*, Management Procurement Division, Headquarters, Air Research and Development Command, March 2, 1961.

Benson, J. W., *Day—Control*, Sandia Corporation, Albuquerque, New Mexico, May 1959.

Brown, Edward A., *Generation of All Shortest Paths of a Directed Network*, IBM Research Center, Yorktown Heights, New York, July 1960.

*Defense Production*, Pamphlet 20-350, Superintendent of Documents, Department of the Army, Washington 25, D. C.

Fazar, Willard, *PERT Time vs. Resources vs. Technical Performance*, IBM Educational Center, Poughkeepsie, New York, March 15, 1961.

Gehringer, A. C., and Kellinger, K. C., *Applications of Line of Balance*, Office of Naval Material, Department of the Navy, Washington 25, D. C.

*Instruction Manual and Systems and Procedures for the Program Evaluation System (PERT)*, Special Projects Office, Bureau of Naval Weapons, Department of the Navy, Washington 25, D. C.

Kelley, James E., Jr., and Walker, M. R., *Critical-Path Planning and Scheduling: An Introduction*, Mauchley Associates, Ambler, Pennsylvania, 1959.

*Line of Balance for Dynamic Management Control*, Light Military Electronics Department, General Electric Company, Utica, New York.

*Line of Balance "Technology,"* Office of Naval Material, Department of the Navy, Washington 25, D. C.

*Lockheed Aircraft Corporation Interdepartmental Communication*, PMS Program Directive 106-59, January 6, 1960.

*Management Data System*, IBM, Owego, New York, January 1960.

Mundorff, George T., and Bloom, William, *Managing a Development Program*, General Precision Inc., New York, 1960.

Norden, P. V., *Observed Regularities—R&D Projects and Their Use in Scheduling Technical Manpower*, IBM, Yorktown Heights, New York, February 15, 1960.

Ohlinger, Lee, *An Operations Research Approach to Budget Control and Reprogramming for the Air Materiel Command*, Computing and Datamation Center, Norair Division, Northrop Corporation, Hawthorne, California.

*Organization of the Special Projects Office*, Special Projects Office, Department of the Navy, Washington 25, D. C., December 20, 1958.

*PEP: Instruction Procedure Skybolt*, Douglas Aircraft Company, Inc., September 30, 1960.

*PERT: A Dynamic Project Planning and Control Method*, IBM, White Plains, New York, 1961.

*PERT Data Processing Handbook for Technicians*, Special Projects Office, Program Evaluation Branch (Sp-12), Department of the Navy, Washington 25, D. C., June 1960.

*PERT Instruction Manual and System and Procedures for the Program Evaluation System,* Special Projects Office, Department of the Navy, Washington 25, D. C.

*PERT,* Polaris Missile System-LSMD, Lockheed Aircraft Corporation, Burbank, California.

*PERT Presentation to Interagency Task Force on R&D Progress Reporting,* The Pentagon, Washington 25, D. C., April 1960.

*Polaris Management,* FBM Program Special Projects Office, Department of the Navy, Washington 25, D. C., (revised) February 1961.

*Proceedings of the PERT Coordination Task Group Meeting,* March 17-18, 1960; August 16-17, 1960; and November 1960; Special Projects Office, Department of the Navy, Washington 25, D. C.

*Production Analysis,* Office of Naval Material, Department of the Navy, Washington 25, D. C., March 1953.

*Program and Management Data System,* IBM, Owego, New York, April 1959.

*Program Evaluation Review Technique: Policies and Procedures Handbook,* Aeronautical Systems Division of Air Force Systems Command, Washington 25, D.C., (revised) January 5, 1962.

*Program Evaluation Review Technique,* Directorate of Engineering Standards, Aeronautical Systems Division, Wright-Patterson AFB, Ohio, September 1962.

*Program Planning and Control System,* Special Projects Office, Bureau of Naval Weapons, Department of the Navy, Washington 25, D. C.

*Program Planning at Link,* Link Division, General Precision Inc., Binghamton, New York, (revised) March 10, 1960.

*Program Planning for Effective Management,* General Precision Inc., New York, 1960.

Rich, G., and Mayte, T., *PERTing by E.A.M.,* Hughes Aircraft Company, Culver City, California, November 1, 1960.

Royar, Admiral M. T., *Navy-Industry Production Analysis-Teamwork Promotes National Defense,* Office of Naval Material, Department of the Navy, Washington 25, D. C.

*Some PERT Definitions Used at LMSD, PMS,* Missiles and Space Division, Lockheed Aircraft Corporation, Sunnyvale, California, August 16, 1960.


## STUDIES


*Activity Definitions for Digital SIN's MK III PERT Flow Chart,* Product Programming, Marine Division, Sperry Gyroscope Company, Division of Sperry Rand Corporation, Syosset, New York.

Archibald, R. D., and Phelps, H. S., *PERT Management Control System Computer Program Write-up,* Solid Rocket Plan, POLARIS Program

Planning, Department 6130, Aerojet-General Corporation, Sacramento, California, June 24, 1960.

*B-70 PEP: Introduction to the NAA Mark I System,* Los Angeles Division, North American Aviation, Inc., Los Angeles, California.

Breitenberger, Ernst, "Development Projects as Stochastic Processes," Technical Memorandum No. K-33/59, U.S. Naval Weapons Laboratory, Dahlgren, Virginia, December 9, 1959.

*Computerization of Manufacturing-Engineering Tooling,* COMET Program, IBM, Owego, New York, October 1958.

Fazar, Willard, "Practical Considerations in Management's Use of PERT," Presentation to Interagency Task Force on R&D Progress Reporting, April 1960.

Fulkerson, D. R., "A Network Flow Computation for Project Cost Curves," Paper No. P-1947, The Rand Corporation, Santa Monica, California, March 1960.

————, "An Out-of-Kilter Method for Minimal Cost Flow Problems," Paper No. P-1825, The Rand Corporation, Santa Monica, California, January 18, 1960.

Hartung, L. P., and Morgan, J. E., "PERT/PEP . . . A Dynamic Project Control Method," IBM, Federal Systems Division Space Guidance Center, Owego, New York, January 1961.

Jarnigan, M. P., *Automatic Machine Methods of Testing PERT Networks for Consistency,* Technical Memorandum K-24/60, U.S. Naval Weapons Laboratory, Dahlgren, Virginia, August 1960.

Larsen, R. P., Program Evaluation and Review Technique (PERT) Formulated for Digital Computer Application," Technical Information Series R60EML48, Light Military Electronics Department, General Electric Company, Utica, New York.

Lasser, Daniel J., *Programmer's Guide to PERT, Phase One for the IBM Type 709/7090 as Installed by POLARIS Missile System,* Missiles and Space Division, Lockheed Aircraft Corporation, Sunnyvale, California, August 29, 1960.

"The Line of Balance as Applied to Production Analysis—Two Case Studies: Assembly Line Production and a Job-Shop Operation," Office of Naval Material, Department of the Navy, Washington 25, D. C.

Maynes, W., *Minutes of the PERT/PEP Computer Implementation Symposium,* Douglas Aircraft Company, Santa Monica, California, December 7, 1960.

Morehouse, W. R., "PERT—An Engineering Program Planning and Analysis Tool," Technical Information Series R59EML63, Light Military Electronics Department, General Electric Company, Utica, New York, September 15, 1959.

*NAVDAC MK 2 PERT Flow Chart Activity Definitions,* Marine Division, Sperry Gyroscope Company, Division of Sperry Rand Corporation, Syosset, New York.

Niemann, R. A., and Learn, R. N., *Mechanization of the PERT System on*

*NORC,* Technical Memorandum No. K-19/59, U.S. Naval Weapons Laboratory, Dahlgren, Virginia, (revised) April 1, 1959.

Norden, P. V., and O'Reilly, F., *Life Cycle Method of Project Planning and Control,* Preliminary Report Paper on a Study Conducted at the IBM Product Development Laboratory, Data System Division, Poughkeepsie, New York.

Pearlman, Jerome, "Presentation on PERT System at General Electric Light Military Electronics Division," Light Military Electronics Division, General Electric Company, Utica, New York, July 1960.

*PERT (Program Evaluation Research Task),* Phase I Summary Report, Special Projects Office, Bureau of Ordnance, Department of the Navy, Washington 25, D. C., July 1958.

*PERT (Program Evaluation Research Task),* Phase II Summary Report, Special Projects Office, Bureau of Ordnance, Department of the Navy, Washington 25, D. C., September 1958.

*PERT (Program Evaluation Review Technique) for the LGP 30,* U.S. Army Biological Warfare Laboratories, Fort Detrick, Frederick, Maryland.

Phelps, H. S., and Chappell, S. A., *PERT Management Control System Computer Program Write-up,* Aerojet-General Corporation, Sacramento, California, (second printing) March 1, 1961.

"Procedure for Preparing TWX Messages for PERT," U.S. Naval Weapons Laboratory, Dahlgren, Virginia.

*Progress in Resources Planning Through PERT,* Technical Information Series R60EML46, Light Military Electronics Department, General Electric Company, Utica, New York, June 15, 1960.

# INDEX